EUROPEAN CHRISTMAS MARKET 2024-2025

Europe's Most Magical Holiday Markets: Crafts, Festive Foods, and Unforgettable Winter Delights

By

Elliot W. Snow

Table Of Contents

Introduction

A Journey Through Europe's Enchanted Holiday Markets

Imagine the air filled with the scent of roasted chestnuts, mulled wine, and gingerbread, mingling with the gentle hum of festive carols. Stalls adorned with twinkling lights offer handmade ornaments, wooden toys, and intricate crafts, each a reflection of the region's history and artistry. In Europe, Christmas markets aren't just seasonal events—they are cherished traditions that bring communities together to celebrate warmth, joy, and wonder amidst the winter chill. This guide invites you to explore the very heart of Europe's holiday season through its magical Christmas markets.

Why Christmas Markets Are So Beloved in Europe

For centuries, Christmas markets have been at the core of European holiday traditions, each one a vibrant expression of regional identity, local flavors, and cultural heritage. Originating in German-speaking regions during the Middle Ages, these markets began as local fairs, allowing communities to gather, purchase winter necessities, and share in the season's festivities. Over time, these gatherings evolved, transforming into beautiful displays of winter cheer, where people of all ages could come together to celebrate the season.

Today, European Christmas markets are famous worldwide for their charm and warmth. From the rustic, wooden stalls of Germany's medieval towns to the romantic, light-filled squares of France, each market reflects its own unique holiday spirit. Visiting these markets isn't just about shopping—it's about experiencing a way of life that cherishes community, history, and hospitality. As you wander through bustling streets lined with festive stalls, sample seasonal treats, and listen to local musicians play holiday tunes, you become part of a tradition that has delighted generations.

What You'll Discover in This Guide

This book is designed to be your comprehensive companion as you explore the best Christmas markets Europe has to offer. Whether you're a seasoned traveler or planning your first European winter getaway, this guide will provide you with everything you need to make the most of your journey. Here's a brief overview of what you'll find:

1. **Insights into Christmas Market Traditions**
   Dive into the history of European Christmas markets and uncover the customs, foods, crafts, and music that make them so special. We'll explore how each country, and often each region, adds its own twist to holiday festivities, offering a rich cultural experience in every destination.

2. **Planning Your Perfect Trip**
   Find practical tips on traveling through Europe in winter, including what to pack, how to navigate crowds, and ways to budget effectively. Discover the best transportation options for hopping between markets, whether by train, car, or plane, and learn how to make your trip as smooth and enjoyable as possible.

3. **The Best Markets by Country**
   Europe's Christmas markets are as diverse as its cultures, and this guide covers them in detail, country by country. We'll take you to Germany, Austria, France, Switzerland, and beyond, highlighting the unique features of each market. For instance, Germany is

known for its traditional crafts and hearty food, while France brings a touch of elegance and artisanal charm. With each chapter, you'll find insider tips on the must-see markets, local foods to try, and handcrafted treasures to take home.

4. **Experiencing the Markets Beyond Shopping**

   Christmas markets are more than just places to buy gifts; they are immersive experiences. From ice-skating rinks and Ferris wheels to live nativity scenes and Santa meet-and-greets, this guide covers the family-friendly attractions and activities that add a festive sparkle to each market. We also feature the best local foods to try, unique souvenirs, and sustainable shopping tips, so you can enjoy the markets to the fullest.

5. **Itinerary Ideas for Memorable Market Tours**

   Planning to visit several markets? This book provides curated itineraries that cater to different travel styles and timelines. Whether you want a week-long adventure through Germany and Austria, a scenic tour of Swiss and French markets, or a comprehensive, multi-country experience, these suggested routes will help you make the most of your holiday.

6. **Winter Attractions Beyond the Markets**
While Christmas markets are the main attraction, Europe has much more to offer during the winter season. This guide includes suggestions for nearby castles, charming villages, ski resorts, and historic landmarks that can enhance your trip. Explore the cultural richness of each destination and create lasting memories beyond the markets.

How to Use This Guide for an Unforgettable Journey

This guide is designed to be both informative and inspiring, helping you create a travel experience that is as joyful and magical as the season itself. Here's how to make the most of it:

- **Plan Your Route:** Start by browsing the "Christmas Markets by Country" section to decide which markets resonate with you the most. Each country offers something unique, so choose the destinations that align with your interests, whether it's Germany's iconic markets or the cozy, intimate markets of Scandinavia.

- **Customize Your Experience:** Use the itineraries as a starting point and customize your journey to fit your schedule, budget, and travel style. Consider adding local events, food tours, or visits to historical landmarks to make your trip more memorable.
- **Travel Mindfully and Sustainably:** Europe's Christmas markets have a deep connection to local artisans and sustainable practices. We've included tips on how to shop thoughtfully, support local businesses, and reduce waste, allowing you to embrace the season with an eco-friendly approach.

In Europe, the holiday season is a time for celebration, community, and cherished traditions. This book invites you to experience these treasured moments firsthand, creating memories that will last long after the lights have dimmed and the markets have closed. Whether you're marveling at handmade crafts, savoring a warm mug of mulled wine, or simply enjoying the festive spirit that fills the air, this journey through Europe's Christmas markets promises to be one of the most magical adventures of your life.

As you embark on this enchanting journey, let this guide be your trusted companion. May it fill you with joy, inspire you to explore, and help you embrace the wonders of the holiday season in Europe.

Chapter 1

Understanding European Christmas Market Traditions

Origins of Christmas Markets: A Tradition Rooted in Community and Celebration

Christmas markets have a rich and storied history that dates back centuries. Originating in the late Middle Ages, they were initially held in German-speaking parts of Europe, where locals would gather in town squares to buy winter supplies and festive goods in preparation for the Christmas season. These markets offered a place for people to come together, celebrate the season, and share in the communal joy that winter festivities brought. As the tradition spread, Christmas markets began to appear throughout Europe, each region adding its own unique flavor, traditions, and specialties.

The earliest known Christmas market, *Decembermarkt*, is thought to have been held in Vienna, Austria, in 1298. However, it was the *Striezelmarkt* in Dresden, Germany, established in 1434, that solidified the idea of the modern Christmas market. Named after a traditional German cake called *Striezel* (a type of fruit bread), the market allowed townspeople to buy holiday goods, food, and gifts, setting a festive tone that would inspire markets across Europe.

Over the centuries, these markets grew from small local gatherings into bustling, enchanting fairs. Today, they are filled with stalls offering everything from handcrafted ornaments to holiday treats, creating a magical experience that draws visitors from around the world.

Traditional Crafts and Artisanship: The Heart of the Markets

One of the defining features of European Christmas markets is their emphasis on traditional crafts. Artisans and craftspeople have long been at the center of these markets, showcasing skills passed down through generations. Visitors can find stalls filled with hand-carved wooden toys, delicate glass ornaments, and intricate nativity scenes—each crafted with meticulous care and a touch of regional character.

In German markets, for example, the famous *Räuchermännchen* (wooden incense smokers) and *Nutcrackers* have become iconic symbols of Christmas. Each piece is made by hand, often in family workshops, and carries a unique story that connects it to the market and region where it was made. In France, especially in the Alsace region, visitors can find beautifully handcrafted decorations and ceramics that blend French elegance with traditional craftsmanship.

Beyond Europe's borders, these crafts have gained global appeal, symbolizing the enduring charm of European holiday markets. They also reflect the values of sustainability and heritage, as artisans use local, natural materials and rely on traditional methods to create lasting, high-quality items.

Seasonal Music and Festive Atmosphere

Music is an essential element of the Christmas market experience, filling the air with the familiar melodies of holiday classics. Carolers, local musicians, and brass bands often perform live at these markets, adding to the festive atmosphere and bringing a sense of warmth and nostalgia. Each region brings its own musical traditions, from the angelic choirs in Austria to the lively brass ensembles in Germany.

One of the most beloved aspects of these musical performances is the *Weihnachtskonzert*, or Christmas concert, which often includes traditional carols, folk songs, and even classical music. Many markets in Austria and Germany have dedicated stages for musical performances, where visitors can enjoy live music throughout the day and evening.

In some regions, unique musical customs add an extra layer of magic. For instance, in Scandinavia, markets often feature traditional *Lucia processions* around December 13th, honoring St. Lucia with candle-lit parades and beautiful choral singing. These musical traditions not only create a joyful atmosphere but also help preserve and celebrate regional holiday customs.

Festive Foods: A Culinary Journey Through Europe's Holiday Markets

No visit to a European Christmas market would be complete without savoring its festive foods. Each country offers a rich variety of traditional treats and drinks that add warmth and flavor to the holiday experience. German markets, for instance, are famous for *Lebkuchen* (spiced gingerbread), *Bratwurst*, and *Glühwein* (mulled wine), a warm, spiced red wine often served in beautifully decorated mugs.

In Austria, visitors enjoy *Kaiserschmarrn*, a sweet, fluffy shredded pancake dusted with powdered sugar, and *Punsch*, a fragrant hot punch made with fruit juices, spices, and sometimes rum or brandy. France's Christmas markets in Alsace offer *Pain d'épices* (gingerbread) and *Vin Chaud* (hot wine) flavored with cinnamon and star anise, adding a French twist to the holiday flavors.

These festive foods aren't just delicious—they are part of the cultural identity of each region. The recipes are often passed down through generations and remain integral to the market experience, reflecting the warmth and hospitality of the communities that create them.

Evolution of Christmas Markets in the Modern Era

While the heart of European Christmas markets remains rooted in tradition, modern influences have brought new elements that enhance these cherished customs. Over recent decades, markets have expanded to include activities like ice skating, carnival rides, and children's workshops, making them popular family-friendly destinations. Markets also host themed events, such as medieval-style markets in some German towns, where vendors and performers dress in period attire, bringing history to life for visitors.

Sustainability has also become a key focus, with many markets making efforts to reduce waste and promote eco-friendly practices. Vendors now use biodegradable cups, encourage reusable shopping bags, and source local products to minimize their environmental impact. These initiatives align with the spirit of Christmas markets as celebrations of community, respect for tradition, and a sustainable way of life.

Another modern trend is the growing international popularity of Christmas markets. Cities outside of Europe, from New York to Tokyo, now host their own versions inspired by the classic European markets, spreading the festive cheer and cultural significance of these events across the globe.

The Timeless Charm of European Christmas Markets

What truly sets European Christmas markets apart is their timeless charm—a sense of wonder and joy that transcends centuries. They are not just markets; they are celebrations of the season's spirit, where people come together to share in the warmth of community, marvel at beautiful crafts, enjoy delicious food, and immerse themselves in the traditions of the holiday season.

For many, visiting a Christmas market in Europe is more than a holiday trip—it's a chance to experience a cherished piece of history and participate in a living tradition that continues to inspire joy and togetherness. As you walk through a snow-covered market square, sipping mulled wine and admiring the festive lights, you become part of a centuries-old story, one that connects past generations with the present and celebrates the universal spirit of Christmas.

In this guide, we invite you to delve into this magical world, discover the history, savor the flavors, and embrace the joy that fills Europe's Christmas markets. Whether you're a first-time visitor or a seasoned traveler, the traditions, sights, sounds, and tastes of these markets promise an unforgettable experience that captures the essence of the holiday season.

Chapter 2

Planning Essentials for Your Christmas Market Tour

European Christmas markets are some of the most enchanting destinations during the holiday season. As picturesque as they are, these winter wonders come with unique travel demands. From packing for chilly days and bustling crowds to budgeting for your market purchases and choosing the best transportation options, a little preparation can make your trip smoother, more enjoyable, and unforgettable. Here's a comprehensive guide to planning your Christmas market adventure in Europe, with tips to help you get the most out of each destination and navigate the festive season's challenges.

Packing for Winter in Europe: Stay Warm, Comfortable, and Ready for the Markets

Winter in Europe varies widely in temperature and conditions, depending on your chosen destinations. However, with layers, essentials, and a few tricks, you can stay warm and comfortable as you explore the markets.

Essential Winter Clothing

- **Thermal Layers:** The secret to staying warm is layering. Start with thermal underlayers for both tops and bottoms to help retain body heat without adding bulk. Look for materials like merino wool or thermal synthetics.
- **Insulated Outerwear:** A high-quality insulated coat or jacket is a must. Consider a water-resistant option to protect you from light rain or snow. Down jackets are popular for their warmth and lightness.
- **Waterproof Footwear:** Comfortable, waterproof boots are essential for walking through crowded markets and possibly wet, icy conditions. Look for footwear with good

traction, as many markets are set in cobblestone squares that can get slippery.

- **Accessories:** A warm hat, gloves, and scarf are non-negotiable. Thermal or touchscreen-friendly gloves allow you to handle your phone or camera without exposing your hands to the cold. A scarf can double as added protection for your face on extra chilly days.

Additional Useful Items

- **Portable Charger:** Between taking photos, navigating maps, and searching for tips online, your phone battery may drain quickly. A portable charger will keep you powered throughout the day.
- **Reusable Shopping Bags:** Many markets are eco-conscious, so bringing your own bag for purchases can be both practical and sustainable.
- **Small Backpack or Crossbody Bag:** Opt for a small bag that can be worn securely and is easy to manage in crowds. Keep valuables like passports and wallets in a zipped compartment.

Navigating Crowded Markets: Expert Tips for Enjoying Busy Festivities

Christmas markets are lively and can get crowded, especially during weekends and evenings. With a bit of strategy, you can make your market visits as enjoyable as possible.

Timing Your Visit

- **Early Mornings and Weekdays:** For a more leisurely experience, try to visit markets during weekday mornings or early afternoons when they are less crowded. This is also the best time for taking photos without the throngs of people in the background.
- **Evening Visits for Ambiance:** If you're after the magical evening atmosphere, aim to arrive just before sunset to watch the lights turn on and enjoy the market before peak crowds arrive. Many markets stay open until around 8 or 9 PM, allowing for evening visits without excessive crowds.

Dealing with Crowds

- **Have a Meeting Spot:** If you're traveling with a group, designate a meeting spot in case anyone gets separated. Christmas markets are often set in bustling squares where getting separated is easy.
- **Keep Essentials Accessible:** In a busy crowd, fumbling for tickets, money, or your phone can be frustrating. Keep essentials like cash, cards, and your phone in an easy-to-access pocket.
- **Take Your Time:** Christmas markets are best enjoyed at a leisurely pace. Take time to browse, sample foods, and watch local craftspeople at work without rushing.

Budgeting Effectively: How to Plan and Manage Your Finances

European Christmas markets can vary in cost, depending on the region and your spending habits. Here are some budgeting tips to make the most of your visit without overspending.

Setting a Daily Budget

- **Market Purchases:** Allocate a daily budget for market purchases. Handmade crafts, artisanal foods, and unique holiday souvenirs are common buys, and it's easy to spend more than planned. Estimate in advance how much you're willing to spend per day on items like ornaments, gifts, and treats.
- **Food and Drinks:** Traditional foods and warm drinks like mulled wine are must-tries at Christmas markets. Budget a small amount daily for food, as many treats are priced affordably but can add up.
- **Souvenir Strategy:** Consider buying small, meaningful souvenirs that won't take up too much space in your luggage. Many markets also offer unique items only found locally, so budget for a few special keepsakes.

Currency and Payment Tips

- **Cash vs. Card:** While many vendors accept cards, some traditional stalls are cash-only. Carry a mix of cash and card options, especially in smaller markets.
- **Local Currency:** If you're visiting multiple countries, ensure you have local currency on

hand. Currency exchange counters are available in major cities, but it's often more economical to withdraw from ATMs or use credit cards where accepted.

Choosing the Best Transportation: Getting Around Efficiently

Europe's vast transportation network makes it easy to hop between Christmas markets across countries and cities. Each mode of transportation offers unique benefits depending on your travel style and destinations.

Train Travel

Trains are an ideal choice for many Christmas market tours, especially between neighboring cities and regions. High-speed rail lines make traveling between major European cities like Vienna, Munich, and Zurich quick and comfortable.

- **Regional Rail Passes:** Some European countries offer regional rail passes that allow unlimited travel within a certain area, which

can be cost-effective if you're visiting multiple markets in one region.
- **Advanced Booking:** Popular routes can fill up quickly, especially during the holiday season. Book your tickets in advance to secure lower prices and better availability.

Driving Between Markets

If you're planning to explore smaller towns or rural markets, renting a car may be the best option. Driving allows flexibility to visit off-the-beaten-path destinations that may not be accessible by train.

- **Consider Weather Conditions:** Be prepared for winter driving conditions, especially in mountainous areas where snow and ice are common. Make sure your rental car has snow tires and consider travel insurance that covers road conditions.
- **Parking and Accessibility:** Check in advance if parking is available near the market locations. Some markets, especially in historic city centers, may have limited parking, so plan accordingly.

Air Travel for Long Distances

For longer distances, budget airlines and domestic flights offer affordable options to hop between countries. Major cities like London, Vienna, and Paris have direct flights to many European capitals, making it easy to explore multiple markets.

- **Baggage Allowances:** If flying between destinations, be mindful of baggage restrictions on budget airlines, as their allowances can be limited.
- **Airport Transfers:** Many airports have convenient rail or bus connections to city centers, making it easy to continue your journey to nearby Christmas markets.

Making the Most of Your Christmas Market Experience

With so much to see and do at European Christmas markets, a bit of planning can ensure a memorable experience.

Plan Your Market Visits by Region

- **Clustered Markets:** Some cities, such as Vienna, Munich, and Prague, have multiple

Christmas markets within a short distance of each other. Cluster your visits to save time and avoid unnecessary travel.

- **Nearby Attractions:** Many Christmas markets are located near historic landmarks, museums, or scenic areas. Consider incorporating these sites into your itinerary for a well-rounded experience.
- **Special Events:** Some markets host special events, such as parades, live concerts, and holiday light displays. Check market websites in advance to see if any events coincide with your visit.

Embrace the Local Culture and Customs

Every European region has its own traditions and customs associated with Christmas markets, so take time to observe and participate:

- **Try Local Delicacies:** Each market has its signature foods. For example, try *stollen* (fruit bread) in Germany, *pain d'épices* (gingerbread) in France, and *jägerschnitzel* (hunter's schnitzel) in Austria.
- **Shop from Local Artisans:** Many markets emphasize handmade, locally produced goods. Support local artisans and take home

a meaningful souvenir that reflects the region's culture and craftsmanship.
- **Learn Basic Phrases:** A few phrases in the local language—like "hello," "thank you," and "Merry Christmas"—can go a long way in enhancing your experience and showing respect for local culture.

European Christmas markets are an immersive way to experience the holiday season's magic and discover the rich traditions that make each destination unique. With careful planning, a sense of adventure, and these practical tips, your journey through Europe's holiday markets will be a memorable experience filled with warmth, wonder, and festive cheer. Enjoy every moment as you explore the sparkling lights, savor traditional treats, and bring home cherished memories from Europe's most enchanting holiday gatherings.

Chapter 3

Germany – Iconic and Historic Markets

Germany is the birthplace of the Christmas market tradition, where medieval charm, festive ambiance, and culinary delights come together in an enchanting experience. From Nuremberg's famous Christkindlesmarkt to the historic Striezelmarkt in Dresden, each German market offers a unique take on holiday cheer, making Germany a dream destination for Christmas enthusiasts. In this chapter, we'll explore the highlights of Germany's most iconic Christmas markets and provide insider tips for visitors to make the most of these remarkable winter wonderlands.

Nuremberg – Christkindlesmarkt

The Christkindlesmarkt in Nuremberg is one of Germany's oldest and most famous Christmas markets, with a history that stretches back to the early 17th century. Known for its traditional atmosphere and high-quality handmade goods,

Nuremberg's market is a timeless celebration of German holiday traditions.

Market Highlights

- **Christkind Opening Ceremony**: The Christkind, a young woman dressed as an angel, opens the market each year with a ceremonial address from the balcony of the Frauenkirche (Church of Our Lady). This tradition sets the stage for a magical market experience.
- **Handmade Treasures**: Nuremberg is renowned for its unique Christmas ornaments, including handcrafted wooden toys, nutcrackers, and intricate ornaments. Look out for *Zwetschgenmännla*, charming figurines made from dried prunes and walnuts.
- **Culinary Specialties**: Don't miss the famous Nuremberg *Lebkuchen* (gingerbread) and *Nürnberger Rostbratwurst*, a small, flavorful sausage served in a crusty roll. Pair these with a hot mug of *Glühwein* (mulled wine) for the perfect festive treat.

Insider Tips

- **Arrive Early for Fewer Crowds**: Christkindlesmarkt is one of the busiest Christmas markets in Germany. Visiting in the early morning or on weekdays will give you more space to explore the stalls.
- **Visit the Children's Market**: For families, the Kinderweihnacht (Children's Market) nearby offers a more child-friendly experience, with a nostalgic carousel, gingerbread decorating workshops, and rides.

Dresden – Striezelmarkt

Dating back to 1434, Dresden's Striezelmarkt is the oldest Christmas market in Germany and remains a historical treasure. Named after the traditional German *Striezel* (Stollen), this market takes place in the heart of Dresden and boasts one of the most authentically festive atmospheres.

Market Highlights

- **Traditional Stollen**: Dresden is famous for *Dresdner Stollen*, a dense, buttery Christmas bread filled with dried fruits and nuts. Each year, the Stollen Festival celebrates this treat with a massive Stollen loaf parade and live baking demonstrations.

- **Wooden Crafts from the Erzgebirge Mountains**: Many vendors sell beautiful wooden decorations, pyramids, and nutcrackers crafted in the nearby Erzgebirge (Ore Mountains), a region renowned for its artisanal woodworking traditions.
- **Historic Ferris Wheel**: Adding to the charm, a historic Ferris wheel offers riders panoramic views of the market and the city's baroque skyline, especially magical after sunset.

Insider Tips

- **Visit during the Stollen Festival**: Held in early December, the Stollen Festival is a highlight of the Striezelmarkt. Watching bakers create a giant Stollen and participating in tastings is a unique and memorable experience.
- **Explore Dresden's Nearby Markets**: Dresden is home to multiple Christmas markets, including the romantic Medieval Christmas Market at the Stallhof and the Advent Market at the Frauenkirche. Exploring these smaller markets offers a

quieter atmosphere and a broader range of experiences.

Berlin – A Blend of Tradition and Modernity

Berlin's Christmas markets reflect the city's eclectic character, offering a mix of traditional and contemporary holiday experiences. With more than 80 Christmas markets across the city, Berlin caters to all tastes, from historic settings to hip, modern interpretations of Christmas cheer.

Market Highlights

- **Gendarmenmarkt Christmas Market**: Set in one of Berlin's most scenic squares, this market is a true celebration of German craftsmanship. High-quality handmade goods, from ceramics to glass ornaments, can be found here, along with live music and performances.
- **Spandau Christmas Market**: Located in Berlin's old town, Spandau Christmas Market offers a more traditional, family-friendly setting with medieval-themed stalls, fire pits, and hearty German food.

- **Winterwelt at Potsdamer Platz**: For a modern twist, Winterwelt offers an Alpine winter sports experience in the heart of Berlin. Visitors can enjoy tobogganing, ice skating, and an après-ski atmosphere, making it a festive adventure.

Insider Tips

- **Combine Market Visits with Sightseeing**: Berlin's markets are spread across the city, so take advantage of this by planning visits alongside major sights like the Brandenburg Gate and Berlin Cathedral.
- **Explore Local Art and Craftsmanship**: Berlin's creative spirit shines at many markets, especially the Eco Christmas Market at Kollwitzplatz, which emphasizes sustainable and eco-friendly products.

Munich – Bavarian Festivities at Their Finest

Munich's Christmas markets are known for their Bavarian charm, local traditions, and beautiful settings. The city's central Marienplatz hosts the main market, but visitors will find additional, specialized markets scattered throughout Munich.

Market Highlights

- **Marienplatz Christmas Market**: Located in Munich's central square, this market is known for its towering Christmas tree, surrounded by stalls selling Bavarian ornaments, crafts, and holiday treats.
- **Mittelaltermarkt (Medieval Market)**: For a unique experience, the Medieval Market on Wittelsbacherplatz transports visitors back in time with historical costumes, medieval crafts, and fire-roasted meats.
- **Christmas Tram**: Munich's Christmas Tram provides a delightful holiday experience as it takes visitors through the festive lights and decorations around the city center while serving mulled wine and Christmas cookies.

Insider Tips

- **Attend the Advent Music Performances**: The town hall balcony at Marienplatz features live Advent music performances each evening, creating a magical atmosphere.
- **Try Bavarian Delicacies**: Don't miss the *Weißwurst* (white sausage) with mustard, served alongside a soft pretzel. Bavarian

beer is also readily available, providing a true taste of local culture.

Cologne – A Cathedral-Backed Christmas Extravaganza

Cologne's Christmas markets are set against the stunning backdrop of the Cologne Cathedral, adding an extra layer of wonder to the holiday atmosphere. Each market in Cologne has its own unique theme and character, making it an exciting destination for variety-seekers.

Market Highlights

- **Cathedral Christmas Market**: The most famous market in Cologne is held right in front of the Cologne Cathedral. With over 150 stalls, this market is famous for its vibrant lights, artisan crafts, and a towering Christmas tree.
- **Old Market (Alter Markt)**: Located in the heart of Cologne's Old Town, this market is known for its fairy-tale theme. The stalls are decorated to resemble houses from German folklore, and you'll find puppet shows and other entertainment for children.

- **Harbor Christmas Market**: Unique to Cologne, the Harbor Christmas Market by the Rhine River emphasizes maritime themes. Look for seafood specialties and nautical decorations, adding a fresh twist to traditional festivities.

Insider Tips

- **Stay Late to Enjoy the Lights**: Cologne's markets are known for their magical evening ambiance, especially around the Cathedral. Visiting after dark allows you to fully appreciate the illuminated decorations and fairy-tale lights.
- **Enjoy a *Kölsch* Beer**: Cologne's famous *Kölsch* beer is served at the markets, adding a local flavor to your experience. Try it with *Reibekuchen* (potato pancakes) topped with applesauce for a delicious combination.

Germany's Christmas markets are an invitation to step into a world of twinkling lights, age-old traditions, and heartwarming food and drink. From the historic stalls of Nuremberg to Berlin's contemporary market flair, each city offers a unique approach to holiday celebrations, showcasing Germany's rich cultural heritage. By exploring these iconic markets with the tips provided, you'll immerse yourself in the magical atmosphere of German Christmas traditions, leaving with memories that will make this holiday season truly unforgettable.

Chapter 4

Austria – Festivities with an Alpine Backdrop

Austria's Christmas markets are renowned for their elegance, alpine charm, and rich cultural heritage. Set against the stunning backdrop of the Alps, these markets transport visitors to a winter wonderland where festive lights, traditional crafts, and delicious treats create an unforgettable experience. From the grandeur of Vienna's markets to the historical allure of Salzburg and the alpine ambiance of Innsbruck, each Austrian city offers a unique take on holiday celebrations. In this chapter, we'll delve into the highlights of Austria's top Christmas markets, including tips for scenic photo spots, local specialties, and insider recommendations for memorable moments.

Vienna – A City of Opulent Christmas Celebrations

Vienna's Christmas markets embody the city's elegance and history, with iconic sites transformed into festive gatherings that exude warmth and charm. Vienna hosts several markets, each with its own character, but the Viennese Dream Christmas Market in front of the City Hall and the market at Schönbrunn Palace are particularly popular.

Market Highlights

- **Viennese Dream Christmas Market at Rathausplatz**: Located in front of Vienna's City Hall, this market is famous for its grand ambiance, with over 150 stalls selling artisanal crafts, ornaments, and holiday treats. The surrounding park is decorated with whimsical lights and themed displays, making it a delightful experience for all ages.
- **Schönbrunn Palace Christmas Market**: Set against the baroque beauty of Schönbrunn Palace, this market is known for its high-quality handicrafts, from hand-blown glass ornaments to ceramic figurines. The atmosphere here is both elegant and cozy,

with classical music often playing in the background.

- **Belvedere Palace Christmas Village**: This market offers a more intimate setting and a romantic ambiance, with lights reflecting in the palace's garden pond. It's an ideal spot for couples or those seeking a quieter experience.

Scenic Photo Spots

- **City Hall at Night**: Capture Vienna's City Hall illuminated with festive lights as a stunning backdrop to the market.
- **Schönbrunn Palace Facade**: The market stalls and palace facade provide a beautiful contrast, particularly as the lights come on at dusk.
- **Belvedere Gardens**: The reflection of the lights in the garden pond makes this a dreamy spot for photos.

Local Delicacies to Try

- **Vanillekipferl**: These crescent-shaped, vanilla-flavored cookies are a holiday staple in Austria.

- **Kaiserschmarrn**: A fluffy shredded pancake often served with plum sauce or applesauce, providing a warm, comforting treat.
- **Punsch and Glühwein**: Austrian Christmas markets are famous for their *Punsch* (a hot spiced punch with a range of fruity and spiced flavors) as well as *Glühwein* (mulled wine), perfect for warming up on a chilly night.

Salzburg – Mozart's Hometown and a Historic Holiday Gem

Salzburg's Christmas markets, with their baroque architecture and snow-covered rooftops, transport visitors to an era of old-world charm. The Salzburg Christkindlmarkt at Domplatz and Residenzplatz is one of the oldest in Europe, while other markets across the city add to the festive magic.

Market Highlights

- **Salzburg Christkindlmarkt**: Located in the heart of the city's historic district, this market is famous for its picturesque setting beneath the Salzburg Cathedral. The market exudes a traditional charm, with beautifully decorated stalls offering handmade gifts, intricate ornaments, and aromatic holiday spices.

- **Mirabell Palace Christmas Market**: Known for its family-friendly atmosphere, this smaller market offers a range of festive activities for children, including pony rides and a visit from the Christkind.
- **Hellbrunn Advent Magic**: Held in the courtyard of Hellbrunn Palace, this market is known for its elaborate Advent calendar facade, where each window of the palace is decorated with festive scenes. The grounds are adorned with thousands of lights, creating a truly magical setting.

Scenic Photo Spots

- **Domplatz with Salzburg Cathedral**: This picturesque location is ideal for capturing the traditional stalls set against the grand backdrop of the cathedral.
- **Mirabell Gardens**: With the castle and gardens illuminated, this location makes for beautiful evening photos.
- **Hellbrunn Palace Courtyard**: The Advent calendar windows, glowing lights, and rustic decorations make this a fantastic spot for festive photos.

Local Delicacies to Try

- **Mozartkugel**: Named after Salzburg's famous composer, these chocolate-covered marzipan balls make for a delightful holiday treat.
- **Salzburger Nockerl**: This airy, soufflé-like dessert is lightly sweetened and dusted with powdered sugar, resembling the snow-covered peaks of the surrounding mountains.
- **Stiegl Beer**: Salzburg's own brewery, Stiegl, offers seasonal brews that are popular at the markets, adding a local twist to the holiday cheer.

Innsbruck – Alpine Enchantment and Traditional Festivities

Nestled in the heart of the Alps, Innsbruck's Christmas markets offer a captivating alpine experience that combines scenic mountain views with traditional Austrian holiday charm. Innsbruck's main market in the Old Town and the Panorama Christmas Market on Hungerburg are particularly popular for their unique settings.

Market Highlights

- **Innsbruck Old Town Christmas Market**: Located in the medieval Old Town, this market is set against the famous Golden Roof, a landmark gilded with copper tiles. The market features stalls selling traditional Tyrolean crafts, hand-carved wooden figures, and ornaments.
- **Panorama Christmas Market at Hungerburg**: For breathtaking views over Innsbruck, take the funicular to the Hungerburg Christmas Market. Set high above the city, this market offers panoramic views of snow-capped peaks and the lights of Innsbruck below.
- **Maria-Theresien-Strasse Market**: This modern market along Innsbruck's main street features contemporary decorations and an array of international goods. The contrast between modern lights and traditional architecture creates a unique holiday atmosphere.

Scenic Photo Spots

- **Golden Roof in the Old Town**: The historic Golden Roof is particularly beautiful when

illuminated and makes for a stunning backdrop.
- **Hungerburg Panorama Viewpoint**: Capture a panoramic photo of Innsbruck and the surrounding mountains, especially magical at sunset or twilight.
- **Maria-Theresien-Strasse**: With its festive decorations and twinkling lights, this pedestrian street offers a picturesque holiday scene.

Local Delicacies to Try

- **Kiachl**: A popular Tyrolean treat, these deep-fried dough pastries are often served with lingonberry jam or sauerkraut, providing a perfect mix of sweet and savory.
- **Speck**: Innsbruck markets feature a variety of Tyrolean speck (cured ham), a must-try local specialty.
- **Jagatee**: A warming alcoholic tea made with schnapps, *Jagatee* is a favorite winter drink in the Tyrolean region.

Tips for Enjoying Austria's Christmas Markets

1. Embrace the Festive Atmosphere

Austria's Christmas markets are best enjoyed by fully immersing yourself in the sights, sounds, and smells of the season. Take time to explore each stall, sample the treats, and enjoy the music that fills the air.

2. Dress for the Cold

Winter in Austria can be quite chilly, especially in the alpine regions. Dressing in layers, wearing warm accessories, and bringing a thermos for hot drinks can make your market visits more comfortable.

3. Try Local Specialties

From *Vanillekipferl* cookies in Vienna to *Kiachl* in Innsbruck, Austria's Christmas markets offer a wide array of culinary delights that vary by region. Sampling these treats is part of the experience and provides a taste of local traditions.

4. Look for Handmade Gifts

Austrian Christmas markets are known for their quality handicrafts, making them an ideal place to purchase unique gifts. Look for items such as wooden ornaments, handcrafted ceramics, and fine textiles as special mementos of your trip.

Austria's Christmas markets, with their historic backdrops, charming stalls, and alpine settings, embody the spirit of a classic European Christmas. Each city offers its own distinct holiday experience, blending traditional Austrian hospitality with unique regional touches. Whether you're exploring the grandeur of Vienna's market at the City Hall, enjoying the baroque beauty of Salzburg, or taking in the alpine views in Innsbruck, Austria's markets promise a festive celebration filled with warmth, joy, and holiday magic.

Chapter 5

Switzerland – Snowy Markets and Stunning Scenery

Switzerland's Christmas markets are like something out of a winter fairy tale, with charming stalls, alpine treats, and snow-capped mountains as a breathtaking backdrop. Known for its picturesque scenery and meticulous craftsmanship, Switzerland's markets offer a blend of traditional Swiss culture, festive lights, and a range of winter activities. From Zurich and Basel to Montreux and Lucerne, each Swiss Christmas market provides a distinct holiday experience. In this chapter, we'll guide you through Switzerland's top markets, including what to see, what to try, and tips for making the most of these snowy wonderlands.

Zurich – A Festive Blend of Tradition and Elegance

Zurich, Switzerland's largest city, offers a magical holiday atmosphere with multiple Christmas markets, each bringing its own flair. The hallmark of Zurich's festivities is the "Lucy" lights display along Bahnhofstrasse, one of the city's main shopping streets, which dazzles with thousands of sparkling lights.

Market Highlights

- **Zurich Hauptbahnhof Market**: Located inside Zurich's main train station, this market is one of the largest indoor Christmas markets in Europe. Its centerpiece is a stunning 50-foot Christmas tree decorated with thousands of Swarovski crystals. Visitors will find a variety of Swiss treats, handmade crafts, and unique gifts.
- **Old Town Christmas Market (Niederdorf)**: In the heart of Zurich's medieval Old Town, this market has a charming, historic vibe with narrow streets and cozy stalls. Here, visitors can shop for traditional Swiss ornaments, candles, and handcrafted toys, as well as

enjoy Swiss mulled wine, known as
Glühwein.

- **Wienachtsdorf at Sechseläutenplatz**: Set
in Zurich's beautiful lakeside area near the
Opera House, this market features a festive
"Christmas village" with stalls selling artisan
crafts, gourmet foods, and holiday drinks. It's
known for its live music performances and
children's activities.

Scenic Photo Spots

- **Bahnhofstrasse Lights**: Capture the
dazzling "Lucy" lights display that illuminates
the famous shopping street.
- **Swarovski Christmas Tree**: The sparkling
crystal-adorned tree inside the
Hauptbahnhof is a must-see and a perfect
backdrop for festive photos.
- **Lake Zurich**: The market at
Sechseläutenplatz offers a picturesque view
of Lake Zurich, especially beautiful at sunset.

Local Delicacies to Try

- **Raclette**: Melted Swiss cheese served over
boiled potatoes, onions, and pickles, a
hearty and delicious Swiss specialty.

- **Luxemburgerli**: A light and airy macaron-like confection, available in many flavors and a perfect sweet treat.
- **Heissi Marroni**: Roasted chestnuts are a popular winter snack in Switzerland and are especially comforting on a cold night.

Basel – A Timeless Christmas Experience

Basel is known for having one of the most beautiful and largest Christmas markets in Switzerland. Located near the borders with France and Germany, Basel's markets bring a unique blend of Swiss, French, and German holiday traditions, making it a must-visit destination.

Market Highlights

- **Barfüsserplatz Christmas Market**: This market is located in the heart of Basel and is renowned for its high-quality crafts and artisanal goods. Stalls offer everything from hand-blown glass ornaments to carved wooden figures, making it an ideal place to find traditional gifts.
- **Münsterplatz Christmas Market**: Set against the backdrop of Basel's historic

Münster Cathedral, this market offers an enchanting atmosphere. Here, visitors can browse Swiss-made products, including candles, jewelry, and winter accessories, while enjoying views of the Rhine River.

- **Christmas Avenue**: This smaller market, located on Claraplatz, offers a more modern twist with a variety of food trucks, vegan options, and a festive cocktail bar.

Scenic Photo Spots

- **Münster Cathedral and Rhine River**: Capture the beautiful market stalls with the historic cathedral and river as your backdrop.
- **Barfüsserplatz**: The market here has a quaint charm, with its narrow alleys and illuminated stalls.
- **Claraplatz Christmas Avenue**: This lively and more contemporary market offers vibrant lighting and a cosmopolitan feel.

Local Delicacies to Try

- **Basler Läckerli**: A spiced gingerbread made with honey, almonds, and Kirsch, it's a Basel specialty and a must-try.

- **Fondue**: A quintessential Swiss winter dish, many markets serve steaming pots of cheese fondue, perfect for sharing.
- **Birnweggen**: A pastry filled with dried pears, nuts, and spices, often served as a sweet snack in Basel.

Montreux – A Lakeside Holiday Wonderland

Montreux's Christmas market is famous for its scenic location along the shores of Lake Geneva. The market offers a unique lakeside holiday experience, with views of the water and nearby snow-covered peaks. Montreux is also known for its "Santa Claus House," located in a nearby mountain grotto, adding an extra magical touch.

Market Highlights

- **Montreux Noël on Lake Geneva**: This market stretches along the lakeside promenade and features over 150 stalls selling Swiss crafts, jewelry, and holiday decor. The views of Lake Geneva and the surrounding Alps add a sense of wonder to the market experience.

- **Santa Claus House on Rochers-de-Naye**: Accessible by cogwheel train, this attraction is located at the top of Rochers-de-Naye mountain. Visitors can meet Santa Claus himself in a cozy grotto setting and enjoy panoramic views of the Alps.
- **Château de Chillon Christmas Market**: This medieval castle near Montreux hosts a small, atmospheric Christmas market with costumed vendors, historical crafts, and seasonal foods in a one-of-a-kind setting.

Scenic Photo Spots

- **Lakeside Promenade**: The market along the promenade offers stunning views of Lake Geneva, especially beautiful at dusk.
- **Rochers-de-Naye Summit**: For a more adventurous photo, take the train up to Santa's House and capture the Alps from above.
- **Château de Chillon**: The medieval castle decorated with holiday lights provides a unique and memorable photo backdrop.

Local Delicacies to Try

- **Filet de Perche**: A local fish from Lake Geneva, often served with lemon and butter sauce.
- **Swiss Chocolate**: Switzerland is renowned for its chocolate, and Montreux markets feature a wide range of handcrafted, festive varieties.
- **Vin Chaud**: Swiss mulled wine infused with spices, similar to Glühwein, perfect for sipping as you stroll the market.

Lucerne – Medieval Charm and Mountain Views

Lucerne's Christmas markets, set against the backdrop of Lake Lucerne and Mount Pilatus, provide a cozy and charming holiday experience. The markets here are smaller and more intimate, offering visitors a chance to enjoy traditional Swiss holiday customs in a scenic and relaxed setting.

Market Highlights

- **Lucerne Christmas Market at Franziskanerplatz**: This traditional market is held in Lucerne's Old Town, surrounded by medieval architecture and cobbled streets. The market features a festive blend of artisan crafts, Swiss winter wear, and local delicacies.

- **Lozärner Weihnachtsmarkt**: Located in front of the Lucerne train station, this market is known for its warm and welcoming ambiance, with vendors selling everything from hand-knitted scarves to local cheese and sausages.
- **Venite International Market**: A unique multicultural holiday market located near the St. Maria church. Here, representatives from around 20 countries showcase holiday traditions, crafts, and foods, creating a diverse and vibrant experience.

Scenic Photo Spots

- **Chapel Bridge and Water Tower**: Lucerne's iconic Chapel Bridge, decorated with lights, is an ideal photo spot.
- **Lake Lucerne and Mount Pilatus**: For a breathtaking view, capture the snow-covered Mount Pilatus with Lake Lucerne in the foreground.

- **Franziskanerplatz**: The market here, with its historic surroundings, creates a charming holiday photo opportunity.

Local Delicacies to Try

- **Älplermagronen**: A Swiss take on mac and cheese, made with potatoes, pasta, cream, and melted cheese, often served with applesauce.
- **Chrabeli**: An anise-flavored cookie popular in the Lucerne region during the Christmas season.
- **Schoggi-Birne**: A dessert featuring poached pears covered in rich Swiss chocolate, providing a perfect balance of sweet and fruity flavors.

Tips for Enjoying Switzerland's Christmas Markets

1. Dress for Winter Weather

Swiss winters can be cold and snowy, particularly in alpine areas. Wear layers, bring warm accessories, and make sure your footwear is suitable for snowy conditions to stay comfortable as you explore.

2. Plan Transportation in Advance

Swiss Christmas markets can be spread across different regions, so planning your travel by train or car is essential. Switzerland's public transport system is efficient and scenic, offering an easy way to navigate between markets.

3. Try Local Specialties

Each market offers regional delicacies that highlight Swiss flavors and traditions. Don't miss out on trying raclette, fondue, and Swiss chocolates that are freshly made and unique to each area.

4. Look for Authentic Swiss Gifts

Switzerland is known for high-quality craftsmanship, from intricate Swiss watches to handmade ornaments. Christmas markets provide a wonderful opportunity to find unique, locally crafted gifts and souvenirs.

Switzerland's Christmas markets offer a truly magical holiday experience, combining festive markets with stunning alpine landscapes and a warm, welcoming ambiance.

Chapter 6

France – Holiday Romance and French Flair

France's Christmas markets exude a romantic charm with a distinctively French touch. From the "Capital of Christmas" in Strasbourg to the enchanting lights of Paris and the fairytale-like atmosphere of Colmar, France's holiday markets offer a magical experience steeped in history, culture, and culinary delights. French Christmas markets combine festive traditions with elegant displays, delicious seasonal treats, and a warm, inviting atmosphere. In this chapter, we'll explore France's most beloved holiday markets, highlighting what makes each one special, where to find unique local delicacies, and tips for discovering hidden gems.

Strasbourg – The Capital of Christmas

Strasbourg, often called the "Capital of Christmas," is home to one of Europe's oldest and most famous Christmas markets. With roots dating back to 1570, Strasbourg's markets retain a strong sense of tradition, blending Alsatian customs with a festive French spirit. The markets in Strasbourg are spread across the city's historic center, with each offering something unique to experience.

Market Highlights

- **Christkindelsmärik at Place Broglie**: This is Strasbourg's main market and a must-visit for anyone exploring the city. The Christkindelsmärik is filled with over 300 wooden stalls offering a wide variety of artisanal crafts, Christmas ornaments, and Alsatian treats like *bredele* (traditional Christmas cookies).
- **Place de la Cathédrale**: Located near the iconic Strasbourg Cathedral, this market offers a picturesque setting with stunning views of the cathedral illuminated at night. Stalls here feature handmade decorations, ornaments, and local handicrafts.

- **Place Kléber**: Known for its massive Christmas tree, Place Kléber is the heart of Strasbourg's holiday celebrations. The towering, decorated tree is a symbol of the market and a perfect spot for festive photos.

Scenic Photo Spots

- **Strasbourg Cathedral**: Capture the beauty of the market stalls with the Gothic cathedral as a backdrop, especially stunning during the evening when it's illuminated.
- **Place Kléber Christmas Tree**: The towering Christmas tree is a must-see and a great place for memorable holiday photos.
- **Petite France**: The historic Petite France neighborhood, with its half-timbered houses and charming canals, is particularly enchanting during the holiday season.

Local Delicacies to Try

- **Vin Chaud**: French mulled wine infused with spices, often including cinnamon, star anise, and cloves. Strasbourg's vin chaud is renowned and can be found at various stalls throughout the markets.
- **Flammekueche**: A thin, crispy tart topped with cream, onions, and bacon, this Alsatian

specialty is similar to a pizza and makes for a savory holiday treat.

- **Bredele**: Small, spiced Christmas cookies that come in various shapes and flavors, bredele are a local holiday favorite in Alsace.

Paris – The City of Lights and Holiday Splendor

Paris, known for its romantic allure, transforms into a sparkling holiday wonderland each December. With a range of Christmas markets spread across the city, Paris offers a unique blend of traditional and modern holiday celebrations. From the elegant Champs-Élysées to the charming Montmartre district, Paris's markets add a festive charm to the city's iconic landmarks.

Market Highlights

- **La Magie de Noël at Tuileries Garden**: Located near the Louvre, this market is one of the largest in Paris, featuring an array of holiday stalls, an ice skating rink, and a Ferris wheel that offers panoramic views of the city. Visitors can shop for handmade crafts, jewelry, and French delicacies, making it a must-visit for holiday shoppers.

- **Champs-Élysées Christmas Market**: This iconic market runs along the famous Champs-Élysées boulevard, lined with wooden chalets selling everything from handcrafted gifts to gourmet food. Visitors can enjoy festive treats while taking in the stunning views of the Arc de Triomphe illuminated with holiday lights.
- **Montmartre Christmas Village**: Nestled near the Sacré-Cœur Basilica, this smaller, more intimate market captures the bohemian charm of Montmartre. Here, visitors can find artisanal goods, local artworks, and cozy cafés offering warm drinks and pastries.

Scenic Photo Spots

- **Eiffel Tower and Trocadéro Gardens**: Capture the beauty of Paris's holiday lights with the Eiffel Tower as a dramatic backdrop.
- **Champs-Élysées Lights**: The Champs-Élysées boulevard, lined with twinkling lights and holiday stalls, offers a breathtaking view that's especially magical at night.
- **Sacré-Cœur and Montmartre**: Montmartre's market, with its cobbled streets and

charming stalls, provides an idyllic setting for holiday photos.

Local Delicacies to Try

- **Macarons**: Parisian macarons in seasonal flavors like chestnut, cinnamon, and chocolate make a delightful holiday treat.
- **Foie Gras**: A luxurious French delicacy often enjoyed during the holiday season, served in various forms at many of Paris's markets.
- **Crêpes**: Warm, freshly made crêpes filled with Nutella, fruit, or savory ingredients are a must-try street food at Paris's Christmas markets.

Colmar – A Fairytale Christmas Experience

Located in the Alsace region, Colmar's Christmas markets are famous for their fairytale-like ambiance. With cobblestone streets, half-timbered houses, and canals, Colmar looks like it was plucked straight out of a storybook. During the holiday season, the entire town is adorned with festive lights, creating a magical setting that attracts visitors from around the world.

Market Highlights

- **Place des Dominicains**: This charming market is set near the Dominican Church, with stalls offering handmade crafts, ornaments, and local wines. The warm glow of the market lights, coupled with Colmar's historic architecture, creates a cozy holiday atmosphere.
- **Place de l'Ancienne Douane**: Known for its scenic location by the canal, this market features stalls selling a mix of regional products, crafts, and holiday decor. The historic Koïfhus building adds to the market's medieval charm.
- **Little Venice Market (Petite Venise)**: Located in Colmar's Petite Venise district, this market is perfect for families, with a dedicated children's area featuring festive activities, mini rides, and holiday-themed entertainment.

Scenic Photo Spots

- **Petite Venise**: Colmar's "Little Venice" neighborhood, with its picturesque canals and colorful houses, is especially enchanting during the holiday season.

- **Koïfhus and Place de l'Ancienne Douane**:
  Capture the beauty of the market stalls
  against the backdrop of the medieval
  Koïfhus building.
- **Place des Dominicains**: The Dominican
  Church and the surrounding market area
  make for an idyllic, storybook-like photo
  setting.

Local Delicacies to Try

- **Pain d'Épices**: A spiced gingerbread loaf,
  often decorated for the holidays, is a
  specialty in the Alsace region.
- **Choucroute Garnie**: This hearty dish of
  sauerkraut served with sausages and meats
  is a local favorite and can be found in
  various Alsatian markets.
- **Kugelhopf**: A soft, yeasted cake with
  almonds and raisins, traditionally baked in a
  distinctive circular mold, making it a delicious
  and unique treat.

Tips for Enjoying France's Christmas Markets

1. Embrace the French Holiday Spirit

France's Christmas markets celebrate the essence of "joie de vivre" – the joy of living. Take time to savor the food, explore artisanal crafts, and enjoy the music and lights that fill each market. French markets are as much about experiencing the ambiance as they are about shopping.

2. Plan for Crowds and Peak Times

French Christmas markets, especially in popular cities like Paris and Strasbourg, can be crowded, particularly in the evenings and on weekends. Visiting during weekdays or early in the day may offer a more relaxed experience.

3. Try Local Wines and Mulled Drinks

French Christmas markets offer a variety of mulled wines and regional beverages. Alsace, in particular, is known for its *vin chaud*, which often incorporates local spices. Don't hesitate to try the local wine varieties and holiday cocktails.

4. Seek Out Regional Specialties

Each market in France offers regional foods and treats that reflect the local culture. Whether it's Alsatian bredele in Strasbourg, macarons in Paris, or gingerbread in Colmar, French markets are a wonderful opportunity to taste unique holiday flavors.

From the enchanting lights of Paris to the historical markets of Strasbourg and the fairytale streets of Colmar, France's Christmas markets offer a holiday experience rich in romance, tradition, and French flair. Each market celebrates the season with its own unique touches, bringing to life the magic of Christmas in one of the most beautiful regions in the world.

Chapter 7

United Kingdom – Historic Festivities and Modern Cheer

The United Kingdom brings a distinct charm to its Christmas markets, combining centuries-old traditions with a vibrant modern flair. Across the country, each city has its own unique take on the festive season, from historic Bath to the lively streets of London and the magical ambiance of Edinburgh. British Christmas markets are known for their variety of seasonal treats, handcrafted gifts, and festive activities, creating a warm and inviting atmosphere for visitors of all ages. This chapter will guide you through the must-visit markets in the UK, each with its own special appeal, local delicacies, and practical tips for making the most of your holiday experience.

Bath Christmas Market – A Historic Gem

Nestled in the heart of this UNESCO World Heritage city, Bath's Christmas Market is celebrated for its picturesque setting among the city's Georgian architecture. The market's charming wooden chalets line the streets surrounding Bath Abbey and the Roman Baths, creating a truly magical holiday experience. Bath's market is unique for its focus on locally sourced and handmade goods, making it the perfect destination for those seeking one-of-a-kind gifts and authentic British crafts.

Market Highlights

- **Handmade Gifts**: Bath Christmas Market emphasizes local craftsmanship, with vendors offering unique items like hand-blown glass ornaments, organic skincare products, and artisanal jewelry. Each stall showcases the talent of regional artisans, giving visitors the opportunity to purchase meaningful, locally crafted gifts.
- **Bath Abbey**: The stunning Bath Abbey provides a breathtaking backdrop, especially when illuminated at night. Choirs and

musicians often perform near the abbey, adding to the festive atmosphere.
- **Victorian Carousel and Rides**: Bath's Christmas Market features traditional fairground rides, including a charming Victorian carousel that's perfect for families and nostalgic visitors alike.

Scenic Photo Spots

- **Bath Abbey at Night**: Capture the beauty of the illuminated abbey with market stalls in the foreground for a picture-perfect holiday memory.
- **Roman Baths**: Just steps from the market, the historic Roman Baths are lit up during the evening, providing an enchanting view.
- **Pulteney Bridge**: Walk to nearby Pulteney Bridge for a classic shot of Bath's Georgian architecture with holiday decorations.

Local Delicacies to Try

- **Mulled Somerset Cider**: A British twist on the traditional mulled wine, Somerset cider is warmed and spiced, offering a comforting drink unique to the region.

- **Hot Chestnuts**: Roasted chestnuts are a classic British Christmas snack, perfect for warming up as you explore the market.
- **Bath Buns**: A local delicacy, Bath buns are soft, sweet rolls sprinkled with sugar crystals, often enjoyed with a cup of tea.

Edinburgh Christmas Market – A Festive Wonderland

Set against the dramatic backdrop of Edinburgh Castle, the Edinburgh Christmas Market transforms the city into a winter wonderland. Known for its extensive attractions and lively atmosphere, this market is a highlight of the city's seasonal celebrations. From European-inspired treats to Scottish crafts, Edinburgh's market captures the spirit of the holidays with a mix of traditional and modern elements.

Market Highlights

- **East Princes Street Gardens**: The main market area, located in East Princes Street Gardens, is packed with wooden chalets offering everything from artisan crafts to holiday decorations and festive food.

- **Ice Skating and Amusements**: Edinburgh's Christmas Market includes an outdoor ice skating rink and thrilling rides like the Star Flyer and the Christmas Tree Maze, providing fun for families and thrill-seekers alike.
- **Scottish Artisan Goods**: Find unique Scottish items like cashmere scarves, woolen blankets, and shortbread, perfect for holiday gifts and keepsakes.

Scenic Photo Spots

- **Edinburgh Castle**: Capture the beauty of the market with Edinburgh Castle lit up in the background, a breathtaking sight especially at dusk.
- **Scott Monument**: This Gothic tower, near the market, offers an ideal vantage point for panoramic views of Edinburgh's holiday lights.
- **East Princes Street Gardens at Night**: The gardens, filled with lights, decorations, and festive stalls, make for a beautifully illuminated photo spot.

Local Delicacies to Try

- **Scottish Tablet**: A traditional Scottish sweet, similar to fudge but with a crumbly texture, this treat is a must-try for anyone with a sweet tooth.
- **Haggis Bon Bons**: These bite-sized versions of Scotland's famous haggis are often served fried, making them a popular and accessible way to try this unique dish.
- **Mulled Irn-Bru**: A playful twist on mulled wine, mulled Irn-Bru is a non-alcoholic spiced drink based on Scotland's beloved orange soda.

London Winter Wonderland – A Grand Holiday Extravaganza

Held in Hyde Park, London's Winter Wonderland is one of the largest and most popular Christmas events in the UK, drawing millions of visitors each year. With a wide range of attractions, from Christmas markets to circus shows and roller coasters, Winter Wonderland offers a holiday experience like no other. The festive market, inspired by German traditions, features over 100 stalls filled with gifts, decorations, and treats from around the world.

Market Highlights

- **German Christmas Market**: Inspired by the famous German markets, Hyde Park's Winter Wonderland features stalls with handmade gifts, Christmas ornaments, and delicious foods from Germany and beyond.
- **The Bavarian Village**: A lively area with German-style beer halls, the Bavarian Village serves up classic German fare like bratwurst, pretzels, and Bavarian beer, complete with live music and entertainment.
- **Santa Land**: A dedicated area for families with younger children, Santa Land includes a Santa's Grotto, family-friendly rides, and festive games.

Scenic Photo Spots

- **Winter Wonderland Entrance Arch**: Capture the excitement of entering Winter Wonderland with its grand, illuminated entrance arch.
- **Ice Kingdom**: This ice-sculpture exhibit features breathtaking ice creations, providing a perfect backdrop for unique holiday photos.

- **Hyde Park at Night**: The entire park is beautifully decorated with festive lights, creating a magical evening atmosphere.

Local Delicacies to Try

- **Yorkshire Pudding Wraps**: A British twist on street food, these wraps feature roast meats and vegetables wrapped in a Yorkshire pudding, a beloved British side dish.
- **Mince Pies**: A classic British holiday treat, mince pies are small, sweet pastries filled with dried fruits and spices, perfect for enjoying with mulled wine or cider.
- **Roasted Chestnuts and Mulled Wine**: Both are market staples across the UK, providing warmth and holiday flavor on a chilly evening.

Practical Tips for Navigating UK Christmas Markets

1. Plan for Cold and Damp Weather

The UK's winter weather can be unpredictable, with chilly temperatures, rain, and sometimes snow. Dress warmly in layers, wear waterproof clothing, and bring an umbrella to stay comfortable while exploring the outdoor markets.

2. Visit During Weekdays and Off-Peak Times

Popular markets, particularly London's Winter Wonderland and Edinburgh's Christmas Market, can become extremely crowded, especially on weekends and evenings. Consider visiting during weekdays or earlier in the day to enjoy a more relaxed experience.

3. Bring Cash for Smaller Vendors

While most major stalls accept cards, some smaller vendors may prefer cash, particularly at local markets like Bath. Bringing some cash can help ensure smooth transactions.

4. Take Public Transport

Cities like London and Edinburgh offer convenient public transportation options, and taking the bus or train can save time and help you avoid parking hassles. Most markets are located centrally, making them easy to access by public transit.

5. Explore Beyond the Main Markets

Each city often hosts smaller, lesser-known markets that provide a more intimate and unique experience. In London, for example, you'll find holiday markets in places like Leicester Square and Greenwich, offering their own distinctive ambiance and local charm.

From the quaint streets of Bath to the bustling lights of London and the enchanting landscape of Edinburgh, the United Kingdom's Christmas markets offer a festive journey through British culture, tradition, and holiday cheer. Each destination brings something special to the season, inviting visitors to experience the warmth and charm of British holiday festivities.

Chapter 8

Eastern Europe – Timeless Charm and Festive Spirit

Eastern Europe is known for its rich cultural heritage, deep-rooted holiday traditions, and enchanting Christmas markets that bring out the true spirit of the season. With cobbled streets, centuries-old architecture, and a wintry backdrop, cities like Prague, Kraków, and Budapest offer some of Europe's most captivating holiday experiences. This chapter explores the unique aspects of Eastern Europe's Christmas markets, from traditional crafts and culinary specialties to warm seasonal drinks and cultural highlights that immerse visitors in the festive charm of the region.

Prague, Czech Republic – A Fairytale Christmas Market

Prague's Christmas market, located in the heart of the Old Town Square, is a magical experience, combining the city's historic Gothic architecture with vibrant holiday decorations. The market's backdrop, featuring the iconic spires of the Church of Our Lady before Týn and the famous Astronomical Clock, enhances the enchanting atmosphere, making Prague feel like a scene from a holiday storybook.

Market Highlights

- **Traditional Czech Crafts**: Prague's Christmas market is famous for its selection of handcrafted items, such as intricately painted ornaments, wooden toys, and marionettes. Visitors can also find delicate Czech crystal and Bohemian glassware, making for meaningful and beautiful gifts.
- **Nativity Scene**: The centerpiece of the market is a large, traditional nativity scene with life-sized wooden figures, often accompanied by live animals like sheep and donkeys, adding a heartwarming touch.

- **Giant Christmas Tree**: Each year, a massive Christmas tree is brought in from the forests of the Czech Republic, standing tall in the center of the market. The tree is beautifully decorated and illuminated with thousands of lights, creating a spectacular focal point for holiday photos.

Local Delicacies to Try

- **Trdelník**: A popular Czech treat, trdelník is a sweet, doughy pastry rolled in cinnamon sugar, often filled with whipped cream or Nutella. The smell alone is enough to draw you to the stalls selling this tasty delight.
- **Svařák (Mulled Wine)**: Czech mulled wine, known as svařák, is infused with spices and served hot, perfect for warming up as you stroll through the market.
- **Pražská Šunka (Prague Ham)**: Roasted on open flames, Prague ham is a savory snack that embodies Czech holiday flavors. It's often served with rye bread and mustard.

Scenic Photo Spots

- **Old Town Square at Night**: With its Gothic architecture and festive lights, the square is breathtaking after dark, making it ideal for capturing the essence of a Prague Christmas.

- **Astronomical Clock**: Located on the Old Town Hall, the Astronomical Clock is a masterpiece and one of Prague's top attractions, beautifully decorated during the holiday season.
- **Charles Bridge**: While not directly part of the market, a winter stroll across the Charles Bridge offers stunning views of Prague's festive lights and is perfect for holiday photos.

Kraków, Poland – Medieval Magic and Holiday Cheer

Kraków's Christmas market, held in the historic Rynek Główny (Main Market Square), exudes a traditional Polish charm that is both enchanting and welcoming. The market brings together local artisans, food vendors, and musicians in a celebration that honors Polish culture and holiday customs, all set within the grandeur of one of Europe's largest medieval squares.

Market Highlights

- **Handcrafted Polish Ornaments**: Known for their intricate designs, Polish Christmas ornaments are often made from glass or hand-painted with traditional patterns, making for a beautiful keepsake from Kraków.
- **Wooden Highlander Crafts**: Stalls feature handmade crafts from the Tatra Mountains region, including wooden figurines, woolen scarves, and intricate lacework that reflect Poland's highlander heritage.
- **Horse-Drawn Carriages**: A charming addition to the market, horse-drawn carriages decorated with holiday garlands offer scenic rides around the square, creating a magical, old-world experience.

Local Delicacies to Try

- **Oscypek**: This smoked cheese from the Tatra Mountains is a regional favorite, often served warm and topped with cranberry sauce for a unique sweet-and-savory taste.
- **Pierogi**: A Polish classic, pierogi are dumplings filled with ingredients like potatoes, cheese, and mushrooms. Some

stalls offer sweet pierogi with fillings like blueberries and sweet cream.
- **Grzaniec Galicyjski**: A Polish version of mulled wine, this warm drink is made with spices, orange, and honey, adding a delicious twist to a holiday classic.

Scenic Photo Spots

- **Rynek Główny at Dusk**: The Main Market Square, adorned with festive lights and decorations, is especially photogenic at twilight, when the lights begin to twinkle against the medieval backdrop.
- **St. Mary's Basilica**: The Gothic towers of St. Mary's Basilica, adorned with holiday lights, provide a beautiful setting for photos.
- **Cloth Hall (Sukiennice)**: This Renaissance structure, located in the center of the square, is beautifully illuminated and surrounded by market stalls, making it a picturesque scene.

Budapest, Hungary – Festive Lights on the Danube

Budapest's Christmas markets, held in Vörösmarty Square and around St. Stephen's Basilica, are known for their festive lights, live performances, and unique blend of Hungarian and European holiday traditions. With the Danube River in the background and Buda Castle illuminated at night, Budapest offers an unforgettable setting for holiday festivities.

Market Highlights

- **Hungarian Handicrafts**: Budapest's Christmas market features authentic Hungarian handicrafts, such as embroidered linens, leather goods, and pottery. Many stalls are run by local artisans who carry on traditional techniques.
- **Advent Feast at the Basilica**: The market at St. Stephen's Basilica includes a light show projected onto the basilica's facade, creating a mesmerizing display of holiday scenes and Hungarian motifs.
- **Free Concerts and Performances**: Visitors can enjoy free live performances, including traditional Hungarian folk music and seasonal concerts, adding a lively ambiance to the market experience.

Local Delicacies to Try

- **Lángos**: This fried flatbread topped with sour cream and grated cheese is a beloved

Hungarian snack and a must-try while exploring the market.

- **Chimney Cake (Kürtőskalács)**: Similar to trdelník, Hungary's chimney cake is a sweet pastry rolled in cinnamon and sugar, often served warm and with various toppings.
- **Forralt Bor (Hungarian Mulled Wine)**: Hungary's take on mulled wine, forralt bor is often infused with spices, citrus, and a hint of honey, making it a comforting drink in the chilly weather.

Scenic Photo Spots

- **St. Stephen's Basilica at Night**: The illuminated basilica, especially with the festive light show, is one of Budapest's most iconic holiday sights.
- **Chain Bridge and Buda Castle**: A walk along the Danube at night offers breathtaking views of the Chain Bridge and Buda Castle, both decorated with festive lights.
- **Vörösmarty Square**: The market in Vörösmarty Square is decorated with holiday lights and ornaments, creating a vibrant atmosphere perfect for holiday photos.

Practical Tips for Navigating Eastern Europe's Christmas Markets

1. Dress Warmly and Layer Up

Winter in Eastern Europe can be very cold, especially in December and January. Layering up with a good coat, gloves, and a warm hat is essential for staying comfortable as you explore the outdoor markets.

2. Try Local Currencies

While some vendors may accept euros, it's recommended to have some local currency (Czech koruna, Polish złoty, or Hungarian forint) for smaller markets or purchases, as it's more convenient for local merchants.

3. Embrace Off-Peak Hours

Eastern European markets, particularly in Prague and Budapest, can get crowded during weekends and evenings. Visiting in the morning or early afternoon can provide a more relaxed experience and allow you to fully enjoy the festive atmosphere without large crowds.

4. Warm Up at Local Cafés

Many markets are surrounded by cozy cafés where you can warm up and take a break from the cold. It's also a great opportunity to sample local pastries and coffee, adding to the cultural experience.

5. Respect Local Traditions

Eastern Europe's Christmas markets are steeped in tradition, and many have long-standing customs and practices. Observing these traditions, such as listening to local musicians or joining in community festivities, enhances the authenticity of your holiday experience.

The Christmas markets of Eastern Europe offer a timeless charm and an immersive holiday experience that blends historic beauty with vibrant traditions. From the medieval square in Kraków to the festive lights of Budapest, each destination in Eastern Europe invites visitors to experience the joy, warmth, and festive spirit of the season in an unforgettable way.

6. Embrace Local Art and Craftsmanship

Eastern Europe's Christmas markets are renowned for their artisanal crafts, with handmade items that reflect the region's deep cultural heritage. You'll find everything from intricate wood carvings and glass ornaments to hand-painted pottery and embroidered textiles. These unique items make memorable gifts and souvenirs, showcasing the skill and dedication of local artisans. In Kraków, for example, look for traditional Polish *wycinanki* (paper-cutting art), while in Budapest, handcrafted leather goods and ceramics are popular. Embracing these crafts not only supports local communities but also brings a piece of Eastern European tradition into your home.

7. Sample Local Specialties and Festive Treats

Eastern European Christmas markets are a feast for the senses, especially when it comes to food. Each country offers its own festive specialties that add to the region's unique culinary landscape. Warm yourself with a mug of *svařák* (Czech mulled wine) or *grzane piwo* (Polish spiced beer), and don't miss out on classic treats like *trdelník* (sweet chimney cake) in Prague, *pierogi* in Kraków, and *kürtőskalács* (chimney cake) in Budapest. These dishes are not only delicious but also provide a taste of each culture's holiday traditions, allowing you to immerse yourself in the festive flavors of the region.

8. Enjoy Scenic Cityscapes and Historic Settings

One of the most enchanting aspects of Eastern European Christmas markets is their setting within cities filled with historical architecture and picturesque views. Markets are often held in medieval town squares, surrounded by gothic churches, cobblestone streets, and historic buildings that add an old-world charm to the festive atmosphere. Prague's market at the Old Town Square, with the towering Týn Church as a backdrop, is one of the most photographed holiday scenes in Europe. Similarly, Kraków's market in the Rynek Glowny (Main Market Square), surrounded by historic townhouses and the iconic Cloth Hall, is both beautiful and atmospheric. The architecture and setting of these markets make each visit feel like stepping back in time.

9. Capture the Spirit of the Season with Local Performances

Eastern Europe's holiday spirit is brought to life through local performances, from carolers and folk dancers to brass bands and live nativity scenes. In many markets, you'll hear traditional Christmas songs in the local language, adding to the cultural richness and authenticity of your visit. Prague often hosts choirs and classical music ensembles, while Budapest features folk music and dance performances, offering visitors a deeper connection to each destination's heritage and holiday customs. Engaging with these live performances is a wonderful way to capture the spirit of the season.

Eastern Europe's Christmas Markets: A Journey Through Time and Tradition

Eastern Europe's Christmas markets are a magical blend of historic settings, cultural authenticity, and festive joy. Each market reflects the local traditions and heritage, from Kraków's medieval square to Budapest's illuminated riverfront, inviting travelers to experience the warmth and charm of the region's holiday season. By embracing the customs, savoring the flavors, and admiring the craftsmanship, visitors can immerse themselves in a Christmas celebration that is both timeless and captivating.

Whether you're exploring the vibrant lights of Prague, sampling sweet treats in Kraków, or watching folk performances in Budapest, Eastern Europe's Christmas markets offer an unforgettable journey through the heart of a region where holiday traditions remain cherished and alive. Let each destination be a chapter in your own story of Christmas magic, as you experience the warmth, joy, and community spirit that make Eastern Europe's markets a true holiday treasure.

Chapter 9

Scandinavia — Cozy Markets Beneath the Northern Lights

Scandinavia's Christmas markets offer a uniquely magical experience, combining a cozy holiday ambiance with breathtaking natural scenery. The festive season in Scandinavia comes alive with crisp winter air, charming lights, traditional crafts, and seasonal delicacies. As the northern lights dance across the skies, Christmas markets in cities like Copenhagen, Stockholm, and Gothenburg bring warmth and joy to locals and travelers alike. These Scandinavian markets provide an opportunity to embrace a unique blend of holiday cheer and Nordic traditions, creating unforgettable moments and heartwarming memories.

1. Copenhagen, Denmark: A Wonderland of Hygge and Holiday Cheer

Tivoli Gardens Christmas Market

Copenhagen's famed Tivoli Gardens transforms into a festive wonderland each December, creating a truly magical atmosphere. The gardens, one of the oldest amusement parks in the world, are decked out in dazzling holiday lights, twinkling beneath the dark winter skies. The market offers an idyllic blend of charming wooden stalls, cozy seating areas, and open fires where visitors can warm up with a mug of *gløgg*, Denmark's take on mulled wine.

- **Handcrafted Danish Gifts**: Stalls are filled with unique Danish crafts, including woven hearts, knitted scarves, and traditional ceramic ornaments. Local artisans display their work, creating perfect gifts and keepsakes.
- **Seasonal Treats**: Savor Danish holiday specialties like *æbleskiver* (pancake balls dusted with powdered sugar) and roasted almonds, as well as freshly baked pastries.

- **Festive Atmosphere**: The gardens feature family-friendly activities, including rides for all ages, Christmas light displays, and occasional performances by local musicians.

Tip: Visit during the evening for an enchanting view of the lights reflecting off Tivoli's iconic lake. Make sure to dress warmly to enjoy the market's outdoor setting fully.

Nyhavn Christmas Market

In Copenhagen's iconic Nyhavn harbor, a smaller but equally charming Christmas market lines the waterfront. Colorful townhouses and historic boats form the backdrop for a cozy holiday shopping experience.

- **Harbor Ambiance**: Stroll through the picturesque harbor and browse stalls offering Danish holiday crafts and locally made goods, such as wooden ornaments and handmade candles.
- **Traditional Food and Drink**: Indulge in hot dogs topped with remoulade and crispy onions, or warm up with a cup of *glogg* as you take in the market's scenic surroundings.

Tip: Nyhavn's market is close to central Copenhagen, making it a great starting point for exploring the city's other holiday events and attractions.

2. Stockholm, Sweden: Celebrating Jul in the Old Town

Gamla Stan Christmas Market

Stockholm's Gamla Stan (Old Town) hosts one of Sweden's oldest and most charming Christmas markets. With its cobblestone streets and historic buildings, Gamla Stan offers an authentic taste of Swedish holiday traditions.

- **Traditional Swedish Handicrafts**: Explore stalls selling handmade crafts, including delicate straw ornaments, wooden figurines, and textiles adorned with Nordic patterns. Artisans take pride in preserving Swedish craftsmanship, and these unique items make thoughtful gifts.
- **Holiday Delicacies**: Try *pepparkakor* (gingerbread cookies), *lussekatter* (saffron buns), and hearty Swedish meatballs. Many vendors also offer *glögg* and locally

produced honey, perfect for enjoying on a chilly day.

- **Festive Events**: Throughout December, the market hosts *Julbord* (Swedish holiday buffets) and special performances of traditional Swedish Christmas songs. Gamla Stan's historic charm and twinkling lights make it an unforgettable holiday setting.

Tip: Visit Gamla Stan on December 13 for St. Lucia Day, when children dressed in white robes and wreaths perform songs throughout the city. This celebration is a key part of Swedish Christmas traditions.

Skansen Christmas Market

Located on the island of Djurgården, Skansen's open-air museum features an atmospheric Christmas market with a historical twist. Traditional wooden buildings and farmhouses set the scene for an immersive Swedish holiday experience.

- **Crafts and Workshops**: Watch artisans demonstrate weaving, glassblowing, and candle-making, or participate in workshops to create your own Nordic-style Christmas decorations.

- **Swedish Foods and Sweets**: Sample traditional dishes like smoked sausage, cured fish, and marzipan confections. The smell of roasted nuts and gingerbread fills the air, making the market feel cozy and inviting.
- **Activities for Families**: Skansen is family-friendly, offering pony rides, sledding hills, and a Santa Claus grotto. Children can meet *tomte*, the Swedish Christmas gnome, and listen to Swedish holiday folklore.

Tip: Spend a full day at Skansen to enjoy both the market and museum exhibits. It's an ideal destination for travelers interested in Sweden's holiday traditions and cultural heritage.

3. Gothenburg, Sweden: A Festive Haven by the Sea

Liseberg Christmas Market

Gothenburg's Liseberg amusement park turns into a magical Christmas village every winter. Known for its spectacular light displays and festive atmosphere, the Liseberg Christmas market is one of the largest in Scandinavia, drawing visitors from across Sweden and beyond.

- **Handmade Crafts and Gifts**: Browse over 80 stalls offering Nordic crafts, jewelry, and gifts. The market emphasizes Swedish traditions, making it easy to find unique souvenirs and locally made products.
- **Scandinavian Foods**: Sample *Janssons frestelse* (a creamy potato and anchovy casserole) and *gravad lax* (cured salmon). For dessert, try *knäck*, a classic Swedish toffee, or *risgrynsgröt* (rice pudding).
- **Activities and Entertainment**: The park offers ice skating, caroling, and visits with Santa Claus. Festive light displays create an enchanting backdrop, and an illuminated Christmas tree stands tall, adding to the winter wonderland vibe.

Tip: Liseberg can get crowded, especially in the evenings and on weekends. Arrive early to fully enjoy the market before it gets too busy, and consider buying tickets in advance to skip long lines.

4. Experiencing the Northern Lights

An Added Touch of Magic

One of the unique draws of visiting Scandinavia during the holiday season is the chance to witness the northern lights. This natural phenomenon, also known as the aurora borealis, is a bucket-list experience for many travelers, and viewing the lights adds an ethereal touch to a winter visit.

- **Best Locations**: For the best views, consider traveling further north to destinations like Abisko in Sweden, Tromsø in Norway, or Rovaniemi in Finland, where you can often see the northern lights on clear nights.
- **Timing**: The northern lights are most visible between late November and March, with peak visibility occurring between 10 PM and 2 AM.
- **Guided Tours**: Many companies offer guided tours that include transport to dark, open spaces where the lights are most visible. Some tours even include dinner and traditional Swedish or Norwegian winter foods.

Tip: Dress in layers, as temperatures can be very low at night. Bring a camera with a night mode setting or consider a professional photography tour to capture the moment.

5. Scandinavian Holiday Events and Traditions

Beyond the markets, Scandinavia offers various festive activities and traditions that add to the holiday charm:

- **Santa Lucia Processions**: Held on December 13, these processions are an iconic part of Swedish holiday culture, featuring children singing traditional songs while dressed in white robes and carrying candles.
- **Norwegian Nisse Festival**: In Norway, *nisse* (Christmas gnomes) are a beloved part of holiday traditions. Cities and towns host celebrations and fairs dedicated to these mythical creatures, where you can find unique gnome figurines and learn about their folklore.
- **Finnish Sauna Tradition**: In Finland, a visit to the sauna is a cherished holiday custom. Some Christmas markets even offer outdoor

saunas, where visitors can experience the warmth of a Finnish sauna under the open sky.

Tip: Embrace Scandinavian customs like *hygge* (Danish coziness) and *fika* (Swedish coffee break) as part of your experience. These small moments of warmth and comfort are at the heart of the Scandinavian winter season.

Scandinavia's Christmas markets and winter traditions offer a magical holiday experience, filled with cozy moments, rich traditions, and unique activities. From the brightly lit stalls of Copenhagen's Tivoli Gardens to the scenic beauty of Stockholm's Gamla Stan, these markets reflect the warmth and hospitality of Scandinavian culture. As you enjoy delicious holiday foods, browse handmade crafts, and witness the northern lights, you'll feel the deep-rooted traditions that make Scandinavia an extraordinary winter destination.

Chapter 10

Italy – Italian Flair and Festive Traditions

Italy's Christmas markets bring a unique blend of Mediterranean warmth, historic charm, and festive cheer, making them a delight for travelers. From the snow-capped Alps in the north to the bustling piazzas of Rome, Italian markets are steeped in centuries-old traditions and regional flavors that make holiday celebrations truly memorable. Italian Christmas markets offer not only traditional crafts and decorations but also a rich assortment of seasonal delicacies, unique local treats, and artisanal gifts. In this chapter, we'll take you on a festive journey through some of Italy's most beloved Christmas markets in Bolzano, Milan, Florence, and Rome.

Bolzano – Alpine Charm in South Tyrol

Nestled in the Italian Alps, Bolzano's Christmas market is one of the most famous in Italy and embodies the unique cultural blend of Italian and Austrian influences. Known as *Mercatino di Natale di Bolzano*, this market is set in Piazza Walther and offers a charming alpine ambiance that captures the essence of Christmas in South Tyrol.

Market Highlights

- **Handcrafted Wooden Toys and Decorations**: Bolzano is known for its high-quality wooden toys, ornaments, and traditional Tyrolean crafts. The stalls are filled with beautifully crafted figurines, nativity scenes, and intricate decorations that make perfect holiday gifts.
- **South Tyrolean Gastronomy**: Bolzano's market offers a delightful mix of Italian and German cuisine, reflecting the region's unique cultural heritage. From cured meats and cheeses to apple strudel, visitors can sample a wide array of festive treats.
- **Holiday Light Displays**: The market is adorned with twinkling lights and decorated

trees, creating a magical setting, especially as evening falls. The lights illuminate the medieval architecture of Bolzano's old town, adding to the festive atmosphere.

Local Delicacies to Try

- **Speck**: A smoked, cured ham that is a South Tyrolean specialty, speck is often served thinly sliced and paired with bread. Its distinctive flavor is both smoky and mildly spiced, making it a must-try.
- **Zelten**: A traditional South Tyrolean Christmas cake made with dried fruits, nuts, and spices, zelten is a holiday favorite that pairs beautifully with mulled wine.
- **Strudel**: The classic apple strudel, with its flaky pastry and warm spiced filling, is a comforting treat on a chilly winter evening.

Scenic Photo Spots

- **Piazza Walther**: The market's main square, surrounded by colorful stalls and illuminated decorations, is the perfect spot to capture the festive spirit of Bolzano.
- **Bolzano Cathedral**: With its Gothic architecture and holiday lights, Bolzano

Cathedral provides a stunning backdrop for holiday photos.

- **Mountain Views**: The snow-capped Alps in the distance add a picturesque touch to any photo, capturing the unique alpine charm of this market.

Milan – Fashionable Celebrations at the Oh Bej! Oh Bej! Market

Milan's Christmas market, *Oh Bej! Oh Bej!*, is held annually near the iconic Castello Sforzesco and dates back to the 16th century. Known for its eclectic array of crafts, gifts, and food, this market reflects Milan's fashionable flair while honoring the city's deep-rooted holiday traditions.

Market Highlights

- **Artisanal Gifts and Crafts**: The stalls at Oh Bej! Oh Bej! offer everything from handcrafted jewelry and leather goods to vintage items and artisanal crafts, making it an ideal place to find unique gifts.
- **Italian Holiday Specialties**: Milan's market features a variety of Italian holiday treats, including panettone, torrone (nougat), and roasted chestnuts. Visitors can also find

seasonal delicacies from various regions of Italy.

- **Historical Atmosphere**: The market's proximity to Castello Sforzesco gives it a historic ambiance, with the castle's medieval architecture providing a striking backdrop for the festivities.

Local Delicacies to Try

- **Panettone**: Originating from Milan, panettone is a sweet, dome-shaped bread studded with raisins and candied fruit. It's an iconic Italian Christmas treat that embodies the holiday spirit.
- **Risotto alla Milanese**: A creamy saffron-infused risotto, this dish is a Milanese specialty that's perfect for a warm, satisfying meal on a winter day.
- **Castagnaccio**: This chestnut flour cake, flavored with rosemary, pine nuts, and raisins, is a rustic Italian dessert traditionally enjoyed during the colder months.

Scenic Photo Spots

- **Castello Sforzesco**: The illuminated castle, adorned with holiday decorations, offers a dramatic and festive setting for photos.

- **Piazza del Duomo**: Milan's iconic cathedral and its grand square are beautifully decorated for the holidays, providing a magnificent backdrop for photos.
- **Oh Bej! Oh Bej! Stalls**: The colorful and diverse stalls of the market are perfect for capturing the lively and vibrant holiday atmosphere unique to Milan.

Florence – A Renaissance Christmas in Piazza Santa Croce

Florence's Christmas market is held in Piazza Santa Croce, where the stunning backdrop of the Basilica di Santa Croce enhances the holiday spirit. Known for its Renaissance beauty and Italian charm, Florence brings a sophisticated touch to holiday celebrations with a market inspired by German-style Christmas markets.

Market Highlights

- **Italian and German Crafts**: Florence's market offers a blend of Italian and German-inspired crafts, including handcrafted ornaments, leather goods, and intricate glasswork. Visitors can browse a diverse selection of gifts and souvenirs.

- **Tuscan Wines and Truffles**: Tuscany's renowned wines and truffle-infused products are available for tasting and purchase, offering a taste of the region's culinary excellence.
- **Renaissance Ambiance**: With the magnificent Basilica di Santa Croce in the background, Florence's market has an elegant ambiance that reflects the city's rich artistic heritage.

Local Delicacies to Try

- **Vin Brulé**: Italian mulled wine, infused with spices like cinnamon and cloves, is a comforting drink to enjoy while exploring the market.
- **Cantucci and Vin Santo**: These traditional almond cookies are often served with Vin Santo, a sweet dessert wine, creating a delightful combination that's perfect for the holiday season.
- **Tuscan Salami and Cheeses**: The market offers a variety of cured meats and cheeses from Tuscany, providing a flavorful sampling of regional specialties.

Scenic Photo Spots

- **Piazza Santa Croce**: The Basilica di Santa Croce, with its holiday decorations and festive lights, makes for a stunning photo backdrop.
- **Florence's Historic Streets**: The narrow, cobblestone streets of Florence are decorated with lights, creating a romantic and festive atmosphere.
- **Arno River**: A stroll along the Arno, especially at sunset, provides a picturesque view of the city's skyline and holiday lights.

Rome – Ancient Traditions in a Timeless City

Rome's Christmas markets offer a unique blend of ancient traditions and festive cheer, set against the backdrop of some of the world's most iconic landmarks. From Piazza Navona to the Vatican's Christmas Tree, Rome's holiday celebrations reflect the city's rich history and cultural significance.

Market Highlights

- **Piazza Navona Christmas Market**: Rome's most famous Christmas market is held in

Piazza Navona, surrounded by baroque architecture and fountains. The market features an array of holiday decorations, nativity scenes, and handcrafted Italian gifts.

- **Vatican's Christmas Tree and Nativity**: Each year, the Vatican erects a beautifully decorated Christmas tree and a life-sized nativity scene in St. Peter's Square, drawing visitors from around the world.
- **La Befana Traditions**: In Italian folklore, La Befana is a kind-hearted witch who delivers gifts to children on Epiphany. The Piazza Navona market includes stalls dedicated to La Befana-themed toys, candies, and decorations.

Local Delicacies to Try

- **Torrone**: A traditional Italian nougat made with honey, almonds, and pistachios, torrone is a popular treat during the Christmas season.
- **Pangiallo**: This ancient Roman cake, made with nuts, honey, and dried fruits, is a holiday specialty that dates back to the Roman Empire.
- **Porchetta**: Roasted and seasoned pork served in a sandwich, porchetta is a savory

Roman delicacy that's perfect for a hearty winter meal.

Scenic Photo Spots

- **Piazza Navona**: The baroque fountains and holiday stalls in Piazza Navona make it a scenic spot for capturing Rome's festive charm.
- **St. Peter's Square**: The Vatican's Christmas tree and nativity scene are must-see sights, offering a beautiful and spiritually significant photo opportunity.
- **Roman Forum and Colosseum**: For a uniquely Roman holiday experience, take a stroll by the Colosseum and Roman Forum, where ancient ruins and holiday lights create a remarkable contrast.

Tips for Navigating Italian Christmas Markets

1. Timing and Crowd Avoidance: Italian Christmas markets can get crowded, especially on weekends and closer to Christmas. Visiting on weekday mornings can offer a more relaxed experience, allowing for easier browsing and better opportunities to interact with local artisans.

2. Sampling Italian Holiday Treats: Italy is known for its regional specialties, and each market offers different treats and delicacies. Sampling panettone, torrone, and regional dishes at each stop provides a delicious way to experience Italian holiday traditions.

3. Dressing for the Weather: Italian winters vary by region, with colder temperatures in the northern markets like Bolzano and milder weather in Rome and Florence. Be sure to dress in layers, especially for outdoor markets in alpine regions, where temperatures can drop significantly. Comfortable shoes are also essential for navigating cobbled streets and bustling marketplaces.

4. Exploring Nearby Attractions: Many of Italy's Christmas markets are located near historic sites and cultural landmarks, making it easy to combine holiday shopping with sightseeing. In Rome, a visit to the Vatican or the Colosseum complements a day at the Piazza Navona market, while in Florence, the stunning Uffizi Gallery and Duomo are just a short walk from Piazza Santa Croce.

5. Embracing Italian Holiday Traditions:
Italian Christmas celebrations are filled with unique customs, from *La Befana* to traditional nativity scenes. Take the time to appreciate these cultural elements by attending local events, watching live nativity performances, or even purchasing a handmade nativity figurine as a keepsake.

Italian Christmas Markets: A Festive Journey of Art, Culture, and Cuisine

Italy's Christmas markets offer an enchanting experience filled with rich traditions, festive flavors, and timeless charm. Each city brings its own flair, from Bolzano's alpine influences to Rome's ancient history, creating a festive mosaic of Italian culture and holiday spirit. Whether you're drawn by artisanal crafts, traditional foods, or simply the joy of the season, Italy's markets provide a delightful way to celebrate Christmas with Italian style. Indulge in the sights, sounds, and tastes of Italy this holiday season, and create lasting memories beneath the glow of festive lights in some of the world's most beautiful cities.

Chapter 11

Spain and Portugal: Southern Europe's Unique Take on Christmas

Southern Europe brings a distinctive flavor to the Christmas season, blending festive traditions with a warm, lively ambiance that sets it apart from northern counterparts. In Spain and Portugal, Christmas markets are infused with the energy of Iberian culture, offering visitors a chance to experience a vibrant holiday season under milder winter skies. From Barcelona's artisan crafts to Madrid's bustling market squares and Lisbon's light-filled promenades, each city celebrates Christmas with its unique charm, where centuries-old customs are met with modern-day festivities.

1. Barcelona: Catalan Flair and Traditional Crafts

Barcelona's Christmas celebrations are rooted in Catalan culture, and the markets here showcase a fascinating mix of Spanish and regional traditions. The *Fira de Santa Llúcia* is Barcelona's oldest and most renowned Christmas market, dating back to 1786. Located in front of the stunning Barcelona Cathedral in the Gothic Quarter, this market is filled with artisan stalls selling traditional Catalan crafts, from handmade ornaments to intricate nativity figurines. Among the most iconic items are *caganers* — small figurines hidden in nativity scenes as a symbol of good luck — a custom unique to Catalonia.

Special Treats and Culinary Delights

Visitors to Barcelona's markets can enjoy a variety of seasonal treats, including *turrón*, a traditional Spanish nougat made from almonds and honey, and *churros* with rich hot chocolate for dipping. At various food stalls, you'll also find roasted chestnuts, or *castanyes*, filling the air with their warm, smoky aroma. This mix of sweet delights and savory street food reflects the region's culinary heritage, giving you a taste of Spain's beloved holiday flavors.

Capturing the Catalan Christmas Spirit

Beyond the stalls, Barcelona's markets often feature live performances, including traditional Catalan dances and music that lend a spirited atmosphere. The *Caga Tió*, or "Pooping Log" — a log adorned with a painted face and hat, which children "feed" and then "beat" to release gifts — is another Catalan Christmas custom that you might see in the markets. These traditions add a playful, uniquely Catalan touch to the festive season, offering visitors an engaging glimpse into the region's culture.

2. Madrid: A Bustling Hub of Holiday Cheer

As Spain's capital, Madrid hosts a variety of Christmas markets and events that capture the city's lively spirit and historic beauty. The Plaza Mayor Christmas Market, set against the backdrop of Madrid's grand central square, is one of the most popular, featuring over a hundred stalls selling holiday decorations, toys, and artisan crafts. Madrid's markets are known for their festive energy, with street musicians and performers creating an animated, joyful atmosphere.

Gastronomic Delights and Local Specialties

Madrid's markets offer a feast of holiday flavors, including *mazapán* (marzipan) and *polvorones*, crumbly almond cookies traditionally enjoyed during the Christmas season. Warming cups of *ponche navideño* (Christmas punch) are also a favorite, often made with fruits, cinnamon, and brandy. These culinary treats reflect the Spanish love for food as a centerpiece of celebration, and visitors can savor these local delicacies while exploring the market's lively ambiance.

Experience Madrid's Holiday Events and Lights

Madrid goes all out during the holiday season, with dazzling light displays across the city and special events like the *Cortylandia* animated show, which delights both children and adults. For those visiting the market at Plaza Mayor, there's easy access to nearby sights such as the Royal Palace and Puerta del Sol, where holiday lights and seasonal decorations create an enchanting winter wonderland in the heart of the city.

3. Lisbon: Festive Lights and Portuguese Holiday Traditions

In Portugal, Lisbon's Christmas markets are a blend of Portuguese tradition and European holiday flair. The *Wonderland Lisboa* market, set in Eduardo VII Park, is one of the city's most popular seasonal attractions, featuring an ice-skating rink, Ferris wheel, and countless stalls offering handmade gifts and festive foods. Lisbon's relatively mild winter allows for a comfortable, enjoyable experience, making it an ideal destination for holiday travelers looking for a warmer take on Christmas markets.

Unique Flavors of Portuguese Christmas

Lisbon's holiday treats showcase the rich flavors of Portuguese cuisine. At the markets, you'll find *bolo-rei* (King's Cake), a ring-shaped fruitcake decorated with candied fruits, which is a traditional Christmas dessert in Portugal. Another must-try is *filhós*, a fried pastry dusted with sugar and cinnamon, often served warm and fresh. Portuguese markets also feature *ginginha*, a cherry liqueur often served in chocolate cups, adding a sweet and festive kick to the holiday experience.

Exploring Lisbon's Cultural Holiday Charm

Lisbon's Christmas markets are often accompanied by concerts, folk dancing, and traditional Portuguese music, adding to the vibrant atmosphere. The city's historic neighborhoods, such as Alfama and Bairro Alto, are beautifully decorated with lights and ornaments, creating a festive backdrop for visitors exploring the markets. With scenic views of the Tagus River and iconic landmarks like the Belém Tower and Jerónimos Monastery nearby, Lisbon offers a holiday experience that combines cultural exploration with festive celebration.

4. Embracing Southern Europe's Unique Holiday Spirit

The Christmas markets in Spain and Portugal bring a distinctive southern European warmth to the holiday season. Both countries blend religious traditions with festive celebrations, and visitors are likely to encounter nativity scenes, or *belenes*, which are intricately crafted and hold deep cultural significance. In Spain, *Reyes Magos* (Three Kings' Day) on January 6th is another highlight, marked by parades and gift-giving, extending the holiday festivities beyond Christmas Day.

Tips for a Memorable Iberian Christmas Market Tour

1. **Plan for Mild Weather**: While winter in southern Europe is generally mild, it can still be chilly, especially in the evenings. Dress in layers to stay comfortable while exploring both outdoor and indoor market areas.
2. **Try Local Specialties**: Each market offers regional holiday foods that reflect local culinary traditions. Don't miss out on tasting *turrón* in Spain or *bolo-rei* in Portugal for an authentic flavor of the season.
3. **Capture the Sights**: Iberian Christmas markets are set against beautiful, historic backdrops. Take the opportunity to photograph iconic landmarks, such as Lisbon's Praça do Comércio or Barcelona's Gothic Quarter, to remember your holiday experience.
4. **Engage with Cultural Events**: From live music and traditional dances to parades and nativity scenes, southern Europe's markets are filled with vibrant cultural events. Joining these festivities will enrich your visit and give you a deeper appreciation for the region's holiday customs.

Spain and Portugal: Celebrating Christmas with Iberian Flair

Spain and Portugal's Christmas markets offer a festive celebration infused with warmth, history, and southern European charm. From the artistic nativity scenes of Barcelona to the dazzling lights of Lisbon, each city's market provides an unforgettable experience that captures the spirit of the season in true Iberian style. The traditions, culinary treats, and lively atmosphere make these markets a joyful addition to any holiday itinerary.

In exploring the holiday markets of Spain and Portugal, visitors can discover a unique blend of cultural heritage and modern-day festivity, where southern warmth and holiday magic create a truly enchanting Christmas experience. Whether savoring the flavors of a Portuguese *bolo-rei* or browsing the artisan stalls of Madrid, each moment spent in these markets will add to the beauty and richness of your holiday journey.

Chapter 12

Belgium and the Netherlands: Belgian Chocolate and Dutch Festivities

The Christmas markets in Belgium and the Netherlands are famous for their cozy atmosphere, artistic crafts, and seasonal treats, offering visitors an unforgettable winter experience. In these neighboring countries, holiday celebrations bring together centuries-old customs and unique, modern twists, with markets set in scenic, historic cities. In Belgium, the allure of world-renowned chocolate and medieval architecture adds to the magic, while the Netherlands celebrates with warm hospitality and vibrant holiday traditions. This chapter takes you through the festive highlights of Brussels, Bruges, and Amsterdam, guiding you on what to taste, see, and savor for a memorable holiday season.

1. Brussels: A Chocolate Lover's Dream

Brussels, the heart of Belgium, transforms into a winter wonderland each year with its celebrated *Winter Wonders* market. Held in the Grand Place, the city's UNESCO-listed central square, this Christmas market is one of the most impressive in Europe, with over 200 wooden chalets offering handmade gifts, artisan crafts, and festive foods. The square itself is adorned with stunning light displays, a towering Christmas tree, and a grand nativity scene, making it an enchanting holiday destination.

Indulge in Belgian Chocolate and Holiday Treats

Brussels is famous for its world-class chocolate, and the Winter Wonders market offers an ideal opportunity to sample some of the finest confections. Local chocolatiers like Pierre Marcolini and Godiva offer an array of holiday-themed chocolates, truffles, and pralines. Be sure to try *speculoos*, a traditional spiced cookie popular during the holiday season, and warm waffles topped with whipped cream or Belgian chocolate sauce. For a festive drink, sample *jenever*, a traditional Belgian gin, often served in holiday flavors like apple and cinnamon.

Capturing the Festive Sights of Brussels

The Grand Place's illuminated holiday decorations and historic buildings create a spectacular backdrop for holiday photos. The light show in the square, synchronized to Christmas music, is a must-see, and the surrounding streets lined with lights and festive stalls offer many scenic photo opportunities. For a panoramic view of the market, consider visiting one of the nearby rooftop bars or restaurants.

2. Bruges: Medieval Charm and Festive Warmth

Known for its fairy-tale charm, Bruges is an ideal Christmas destination, with cobblestone streets, medieval architecture, and picturesque canals that add to its magical winter atmosphere. The Bruges Christmas market is centered in the Market Square, where the city's historic belfry overlooks a festive scene of twinkling lights, skating rinks, and cozy market stalls. The combination of Bruges's old-world ambiance and holiday spirit makes this market a favorite among visitors.

Sampling Festive Foods and Drinks

Bruges is a haven for food lovers, especially during the holiday season. The Christmas market offers a variety of Belgian specialties, including fresh *pommes frites* (Belgian fries) served with a variety of sauces, and *oliebollen*, fluffy doughnuts dusted with powdered sugar. For a heartwarming drink, try *glühwein*, a spiced mulled wine popular in Belgium, or *chocolat chaud* (hot chocolate), made with rich Belgian chocolate for an indulgent treat.

Exploring Bruges by Night

As night falls, the lights of Bruges' Christmas market and surrounding buildings reflect beautifully in the canals, creating a picture-perfect holiday scene. Take a leisurely evening walk along the canals or visit one of the small bridges for a memorable photo of Bruges lit up for the season. The belfry, adorned with lights, serves as a stunning focal point and adds to the enchanting ambiance.

3. Amsterdam: Dutch Festivities and Winter Cheer

Amsterdam's Christmas season is filled with festive events, markets, and light displays that capture the warmth of Dutch holiday celebrations. The *Amsterdam Winter Paradise* market, located at the RAI Amsterdam, is one of the city's largest holiday markets, featuring indoor and outdoor activities, including ice skating, a Ferris wheel, and live music. For a more traditional market experience, the *Ice Village* near the Museumplein offers seasonal stalls, holiday treats, and a cozy ambiance.

Taste Dutch Delicacies and Holiday Drinks

Amsterdam's holiday markets showcase Dutch treats that reflect the country's culinary heritage. Indulge in *poffertjes*, small fluffy pancakes dusted with powdered sugar, or *stroopwafels*, thin waffles filled with caramel syrup. During the holidays, many market stalls serve *erwtensoep*, a hearty pea soup often enjoyed on cold winter days. Wash it down with a warm *bisschopswijn*, the Dutch version of mulled wine, or try *anijsmelk*, a warm milk flavored with anise, for a comforting seasonal drink.

Amsterdam's Iconic Light Displays

Amsterdam's Christmas markets are complemented by the city's *Amsterdam Light Festival*, which illuminates the canals and historic buildings with colorful, artistic displays. Taking a canal cruise during the festival offers a unique way to see the light installations from the water, providing an ideal setting for memorable holiday photos. Whether walking along the canals or viewing the city from a boat, the lights add a magical dimension to Amsterdam's holiday celebrations.

Insider Tips for Enjoying Belgium and the Netherlands' Holiday Markets

1. **Try Local Specialties**: Each market offers seasonal treats and drinks unique to its region. Sampling these foods, from Belgian chocolate to Dutch pancakes, enhances the holiday experience and provides a delicious way to explore local culture.
2. **Visit During the Evening**: The festive lights at night make for a more enchanting atmosphere, and the illuminated buildings

and squares in cities like Brussels and Bruges provide stunning backdrops for photos.

3. **Take Time for Exploration**: The markets in Belgium and the Netherlands are often near historic landmarks and scenic areas. Allow time to explore beyond the market stalls to experience the charm of each city's architecture, canals, and festive decorations.

4. **Plan for Crowds on Weekends**: These popular holiday markets tend to be busiest on weekends. If possible, visit during the week to enjoy a more relaxed atmosphere and shorter lines at popular food and craft stalls.

The Christmas markets in Belgium and the Netherlands offer a festive journey filled with rich flavors, beautiful decorations, and warm holiday cheer. From the historic grandeur of Brussels' Grand Place to the fairy-tale charm of Bruges and the vibrant canals of Amsterdam, each destination provides a unique celebration that captures the essence of the season. Belgium's renowned chocolates, Dutch holiday treats, and scenic backdrops create an inviting, unforgettable experience that showcases the holiday spirit in its finest form.

Chapter 13

Holiday Market Foods to Savor

European Christmas markets are famous not only for their festive atmosphere but also for their array of mouthwatering holiday treats. Wandering through the stalls, you're greeted by the irresistible aromas of spiced mulled wine, roasting chestnuts, and freshly baked pastries. From sweet delicacies to savory snacks, each region offers its unique culinary delights that capture the season's spirit. In this chapter, we'll explore the must-try foods you'll find at Christmas markets across Europe and offer tips on where to find the most authentic and delicious options.

1. Sweet Treats: A Taste of Christmas Magic

Gingerbread (Lebkuchen)

One of the most iconic holiday treats, gingerbread—known as *Lebkuchen* in Germany—is a staple at many Christmas markets. These spiced cookies come in various forms, from soft and chewy to crunchy and glazed, often decorated with intricate designs or festive messages. Nuremberg, Germany, is especially famous for its *Lebkuchen*, where local bakers use traditional recipes that blend honey, cinnamon, cloves, and nuts for a distinct, festive flavor. Look for vendors selling gingerbread hearts decorated with icing, a perfect souvenir or gift for loved ones.

Marzipan and Stollen

In German-speaking regions, marzipan—a sweet almond paste—is a cherished holiday treat often shaped into fruits, animals, or festive figures. Lübeck, Germany, is famous for its marzipan, which is crafted with premium almonds and sugar for a smooth, rich taste. Another beloved German treat is *Stollen*, a dense, fruit-filled bread dusted with powdered sugar. Dresden's Christmas market,

Striezelmarkt, is renowned for its *Christstollen*, made with dried fruits, nuts, and spices. Slices of this festive bread pair perfectly with a hot cup of mulled wine on a chilly evening.

Poffertjes and Stroopwafels

In the Netherlands, holiday markets offer delicious sweets that have become beloved traditions. *Poffertjes* are small, fluffy pancakes dusted with powdered sugar and often topped with butter or syrup. Their light, airy texture and sweet flavor make them a delightful snack for any visitor. *Stroopwafels* are another must-try Dutch treat—thin, crispy waffle cookies filled with a layer of caramel syrup. To enjoy them warm, try placing a *stroopwafel* over your hot coffee or tea for a few seconds, allowing the caramel to melt slightly.

French Pastries and Macarons

French Christmas markets are a haven for pastry lovers. Indulge in traditional French pastries such as *pain d'épices* (spiced bread), similar to gingerbread but softer and more cake-like. Strasbourg's market is a top destination for holiday baked goods, where you'll find everything from buttery croissants to colorful macarons in seasonal flavors. Try the almond-filled *galette des rois*, a flaky pastry typically enjoyed around the holidays. French markets often offer handmade chocolates and pralines that make excellent gifts for friends and family.

2. Savory Delights: Hearty Winter Warmers

Bratwurst and Sausages

No Christmas market experience is complete without tasting *bratwurst*, a German sausage that's grilled to perfection and served in a fresh roll. Germany's markets are known for their wide variety of sausages, from classic *bratwurst* to *currywurst*, a popular choice topped with curry ketchup and curry powder. Nuremberg's small, flavorful *Nürnberger Rostbratwurst* is a local specialty often served three at a time in a crusty bun. Austria's markets also offer unique sausages, like *käsekrainer*, a sausage filled with melted cheese, perfect for a satisfying winter snack.

Cheese and Raclette

Cheese lovers will find plenty to enjoy at European Christmas markets, particularly in Switzerland and France. One of the most popular treats is *raclette*, a type of cheese melted and scraped over potatoes, bread, or pickles. The rich, gooey cheese pairs beautifully with the sharpness of pickles and the softness of potatoes, making it a comforting choice on a cold evening. Swiss markets in cities like Montreux and Zurich are ideal spots to sample authentic raclette, but you'll also find it at various markets across Europe.

Pierogi and Other Eastern European Specialties

In Eastern Europe, holiday markets offer hearty, comforting foods like *pierogi*, traditional Polish dumplings stuffed with fillings such as cheese, potatoes, mushrooms, or meat. You'll find these delicious dumplings served hot, often with a dollop of sour cream or sprinkled with crispy fried onions. Prague and Kraków markets also serve holiday favorites like *langos*, a fried dough topped with garlic, cheese, or sour cream, and *kielbasa*, a Polish sausage grilled to perfection. These filling treats are a perfect way to experience the warmth of Eastern European cuisine.

3. Festive Drinks: Toasting the Season

Glühwein and Mulled Wine

Glühwein (mulled wine) is a quintessential Christmas market drink that brings warmth to chilly winter nights. This spiced wine, typically red, is simmered with ingredients like cinnamon, cloves, and orange peel, creating a fragrant, warming beverage. Glühwein is found in almost every European market, each with its own twist—try white mulled wine in Austria or add a shot of *rum* or *amaretto* in Germany for an extra kick. For a fun souvenir, many markets offer collectible mugs with their own designs.

Hot Chocolate and Anijsmelk

Indulge in rich hot chocolate, a popular choice across European markets, especially in Belgium and France. Some markets serve thick, velvety hot chocolate made from real melted chocolate, topped with whipped cream or marshmallows. In the Netherlands, try *anijsmelk*, a traditional warm milk flavored with anise, which has a soothing, mildly sweet taste that's perfect for relaxing after a day of exploring.

Eggnog and Bombardino

In Italy, especially in the Alps, a warming drink called *bombardino* is popular during the winter season. This creamy, eggnog-like drink is made from a mix of brandy, egg liqueur, and whipped cream, creating a rich, warming beverage perfect for cold nights. For a more traditional taste, try *vin brulé*, the Italian version of mulled wine, infused with local spices and citrus zest.

4. Tips for Finding the Best Market Foods

- **Look for Local Specialties**: Many markets feature regional treats, so take the opportunity to try something unique to the area, like Dresden's *Stollen* or Vienna's *maroni* (roasted chestnuts).
- **Enjoy Foods in Small Portions**: Christmas markets are perfect for sampling a variety of dishes. Opt for smaller portions to try as many flavors as possible without feeling too full.
- **Ask Vendors for Recommendations**: Many vendors are passionate about their products and can offer advice on the best items to try or unique specialties you might overlook.

- **Arrive Early or Late**: To avoid long lines at popular stalls, consider visiting markets either early in the day or later in the evening. You'll have more time to browse and savor each treat.

European Christmas markets offer an irresistible culinary experience, where traditional recipes and seasonal flavors bring people together in celebration. Whether it's the sweet aroma of freshly baked gingerbread or the comforting warmth of mulled wine, the festive foods at these markets are as much a part of the holiday spirit as the decorations and lights. Embrace the opportunity to taste your way through Europe, enjoying the unique flavors that make each market special.

Chapter 14

The Art of Holiday Shopping: Unique Gifts and Souvenirs

Christmas markets across Europe are not only a place to experience festive cheer and savor holiday treats, but also a treasure trove for holiday shoppers seeking one-of-a-kind gifts and souvenirs. These markets are famous for their array of handmade ornaments, artisanal crafts, and delicious edible gifts, all of which bring a piece of Europe's holiday spirit back home. In this chapter, we'll guide you through the essentials of holiday shopping at Christmas markets, with tips on selecting meaningful items, packing them safely, and choosing perfect gifts for loved ones.

1. Unique Holiday Ornaments

One of the most cherished aspects of Christmas market shopping is the variety of unique, handmade ornaments available at almost every stall. These decorations range from delicate glass baubles to hand-carved wooden figures, each reflecting the local culture and craftsmanship of the region.

Hand-Blown Glass Ornaments

In countries like Germany and the Czech Republic, hand-blown glass ornaments are a specialty. Skilled artisans create intricate glass designs, sometimes incorporating traditional holiday motifs like angels, snowflakes, or stars. The town of Lauscha in Germany is particularly renowned for its glass ornaments, with a tradition dating back to the 16th century. Look for clear or colored glass baubles with hand-painted details—each ornament is a work of art that adds elegance and charm to any tree.

Wooden Carvings and Nutcrackers

Wooden ornaments, especially from the German regions of Erzgebirge and Bavaria, are known for their rustic beauty. You'll find hand-carved nativity scenes, stars, and angels crafted from natural wood, as well as iconic nutcrackers and smoking men figures. Nutcrackers are especially popular, symbolizing good luck and protection, and make for a meaningful addition to any holiday decor. For a truly unique piece, look for small, hand-painted wooden ornaments that capture the essence of a European Christmas.

Strohsterne (Straw Stars)

In Austria and other parts of central Europe, straw stars, or *Strohsterne*, are a traditional Christmas decoration made by weaving dried straw into star shapes. These ornaments add a natural, rustic touch to holiday decor and are a wonderful way to bring a bit of European tradition to your home. Straw ornaments are lightweight and easy to pack, making them an excellent souvenir.

2. Artisanal Crafts and Handmade Gifts

Christmas markets are also known for their variety of high-quality, handmade crafts. These items are often crafted with care and attention to detail, making them ideal for meaningful gifts.

Pottery and Ceramics

European Christmas markets offer a variety of handmade pottery and ceramics that showcase the region's artistic traditions. Polish pottery, known for its intricate patterns and vibrant colors, is particularly popular and can be found at many Eastern European markets. These pieces include mugs, plates, and serving dishes that are not only beautiful but also functional. Look for ceramic items with holiday themes, such as mugs adorned with snowflakes or plates featuring festive designs, which make for thoughtful gifts.

Textiles and Woolen Goods

Winter textiles such as scarves, mittens, hats, and blankets are common finds at Christmas markets, especially in colder regions like Scandinavia and Eastern Europe. Handmade from wool or alpaca, these items are often knitted or woven with traditional patterns and bright colors. In Norway and Sweden, you'll find cozy woolen sweaters and socks decorated with Nordic motifs, while in Hungary, you might come across intricate lace or embroidered linens. These warm and practical gifts are perfect for family members and friends who love cozy winter wear.

Leather and Wooden Crafts

Markets in countries like Italy and Switzerland offer finely crafted leather goods, from belts and wallets to keychains and bags. You may also find wooden crafts such as hand-carved figurines, cutting boards, and utensils, which showcase the skill of local artisans. These items are often made using traditional methods and make timeless, durable gifts that can be cherished for years.

3. Edible Gifts and Holiday Treats

For many visitors, edible gifts are among the most delightful souvenirs to take home. These holiday treats bring the flavors of Europe's Christmas markets to loved ones and make wonderful additions to holiday gatherings.

Spiced Cookies and Gingerbread

Gingerbread cookies and other spiced treats are popular edible gifts, especially in Germany, where *Lebkuchen* cookies are a holiday favorite. Look for cookies decorated with festive icing or shaped into hearts with messages of love and joy. Similarly, speculaas cookies, with their distinct spices and almond slivers, are a Dutch specialty that adds a sweet touch to holiday gift baskets.

Stollen and Fruitcake

For those looking to share a taste of traditional European holiday baking, stollen and fruitcake make excellent gifts. Dresden's Christmas market is particularly famous for its *Christstollen*, a rich, fruit-filled bread dusted with powdered sugar. Fruitcakes are also popular in the UK, often baked with dried fruits and nuts soaked in brandy. These hearty treats are a delicious reminder of Europe's holiday flavors and are sure to be enjoyed by family and friends.

Cheeses, Meats, and Charcuterie

Christmas markets in France, Switzerland, and Italy often offer gourmet items like cheese, cured meats, and charcuterie boards, which make luxurious gifts for food lovers. In Switzerland, look for raclette cheese, while France offers creamy *brie* and *camembert*. Be sure to check the guidelines for transporting these items if you're traveling internationally, as some products may have restrictions.

4. Tips for Choosing Meaningful Gifts

When selecting gifts and souvenirs at Christmas markets, it's helpful to keep a few key tips in mind to ensure that your purchases are both meaningful and memorable.

Consider Local Traditions and Heritage

Choose items that reflect the unique heritage and traditions of the region. Handcrafted ornaments, pottery, and textiles that are unique to a particular country or region make for memorable gifts that carry a piece of the culture with them. Not only do these items showcase local artistry, but they also support local artisans.

Look for Handcrafted and Artisanal Items

Handmade items often hold greater sentimental value than mass-produced goods. Whether it's a hand-painted ornament or a woven scarf, artisanal products typically reflect the quality and care of their creators. Take the time to learn about the item's origins and techniques used to create it—many vendors are happy to share the story behind their work.

Think About Practicality and Usefulness

Consider items that are both beautiful and practical. A hand-knitted scarf, a decorative ceramic bowl, or a reusable shopping bag with a festive design are all gifts that can be used and enjoyed year-round, adding a touch of European charm to daily life.

5. Packing and Transporting Souvenirs Safely

Bringing fragile or perishable gifts back home requires careful planning to ensure they arrive safely. Here are some practical tips for packing your Christmas market treasures.

Use Bubble Wrap and Padding

For delicate items like glass ornaments or ceramics, pack them in bubble wrap or cloth to prevent breakage. If you're traveling with a suitcase, try packing fragile items in the center, surrounded by softer items like clothing for extra protection.

Carry Small, Valuable Items as Hand Luggage

For valuable or particularly fragile gifts, consider keeping them in your carry-on luggage. This reduces the risk of them being damaged in transit and allows you to keep a close eye on your most precious purchases.

Check for Airline and Customs Restrictions

If you're bringing food items like cheese, meats, or wine, make sure to check customs regulations and airline policies beforehand. Some items may have restrictions for international travel, so it's best to be aware of these in advance to avoid any issues at customs.

Consider Shipping Large or Heavy Items

If you've purchased large items or multiple gifts, it may be more convenient to ship them directly to your home. Many vendors at Christmas markets offer international shipping services, so ask about this option if you'd like to lighten your load.

6. Thoughtful Gift Ideas for Loved Ones

Here are a few ideas to help you choose gifts that friends and family will cherish:

- **For Food Lovers**: A selection of spiced cookies, stollen, or artisanal chocolates that reflect the tastes of the season.

- **For Art Enthusiasts**: Handcrafted pottery or a set of hand-blown glass ornaments showcasing local artistry.
- **For Cozy Comfort**: A warm woolen scarf or a knitted blanket from Scandinavian markets for snuggling up during the winter months.
- **For Home Decor**: A unique holiday ornament or carved wooden figure that brings festive cheer to any space.

European Christmas markets offer endless opportunities for finding special gifts and souvenirs that capture the spirit of the season. Whether you're searching for beautiful decorations, cozy winter wear, or delicious treats, these markets are filled with items that bring a little piece of Europe's holiday magic back home. With thoughtful planning and careful selection, you'll have gifts that evoke memories of your holiday travels for years to come.

Chapter 15

Family-Friendly Christmas Markets

A trip to a Christmas market is a magical experience for all ages, but for families with children, it can be a particularly enchanting adventure. Many of Europe's Christmas markets have transformed themselves into family-friendly winter wonderlands, filled with activities and attractions that make the season sparkle for young visitors. From dazzling lights and festive music to thrilling rides and encounters with Santa, these markets offer unforgettable moments for children and parents alike. In this chapter, we'll explore the top family-friendly Christmas markets in Europe, highlighting their kid-focused attractions and sharing helpful tips for making your visit fun, safe, and memorable.

1. Highlights of Family-Friendly Markets

Across Europe, many Christmas markets go out of their way to create an experience that appeals to children and families. These markets often include dedicated areas with child-friendly attractions, interactive activities, and cozy spots for families to relax and warm up. Here are some key features to look for in family-friendly Christmas markets.

Santa's Grotto and Meet-and-Greets

Meeting Santa Claus is a highlight for many children, and several Christmas markets offer opportunities to visit Santa's grotto. Kids can share their Christmas wishes and pose for photos with Santa and his elves. Markets in cities like Brussels, Edinburgh, and Vienna have festive grottos where children can meet Santa in a cozy, decorated setting.

Ice Rinks

Ice skating is a favorite holiday activity, and many markets feature large ice rinks where families can glide under twinkling lights. Whether in a picturesque square or surrounded by charming market stalls, ice rinks add an extra layer of holiday excitement. Markets in Paris, London, and Munich are known for their spacious ice skating areas, which are often set against iconic landmarks.

Ferris Wheels and Carousel Rides

Many markets offer classic fairground rides, such as Ferris wheels, carousels, and even small roller coasters, making the experience thrilling for young adventurers. The Ferris wheels at markets like the Hyde Park Winter Wonderland in London and the Christkindlesmarkt in Nuremberg provide stunning views of the festive lights and bustling crowds below.

Craft Workshops for Kids

In some markets, children can participate in holiday-themed craft workshops where they make their own ornaments, decorate gingerbread cookies, or create Christmas cards. These hands-on activities allow children to express their creativity and take home a handmade souvenir. Christmas markets in Vienna and Prague often include such workshops in their family areas.

Live Shows and Puppet Theatres

To keep children entertained, many markets host live performances, including puppet shows, storytelling sessions, and holiday-themed plays. These performances usually take place on small stages or in cozy tents and feature tales of holiday magic and traditional folklore. Families visiting markets in places like Salzburg and Copenhagen can enjoy these delightful shows as a break from exploring the stalls.

2. Top Family-Friendly Christmas Markets in Europe

Let's take a closer look at some of the best Christmas markets for families, each with unique attractions that make them perfect destinations for kids and parents alike.

1. Christkindlesmarkt – Nuremberg, Germany

One of Germany's most famous Christmas markets, Nuremberg's Christkindlesmarkt offers a magical experience for families with its dedicated Kinderweihnacht, or Children's Market. This area features a mini Ferris wheel, a carousel, and a train ride, as well as a playhouse where children can enjoy puppet shows and storytelling sessions. There's even a post office where kids can write letters to Santa.

2. Hyde Park Winter Wonderland – London, United Kingdom

Hyde Park's Winter Wonderland is a sprawling holiday event that offers a range of family-friendly attractions. In addition to a massive ice rink, the park features a circus, an ice sculpture exhibition, and a Santa Land with rides and games. The Giant Observation Wheel offers panoramic views over London, and kids will love exploring the Magical Ice Kingdom, an enchanting display of ice sculptures and winter scenes.

3. Wiener Christkindlmarkt – Vienna, Austria

Vienna's main Christmas market, located in front of the City Hall, offers a dedicated children's area with craft workshops, where kids can decorate cookies and make Christmas ornaments. The market also has a beautiful ice rink and special storytelling sessions inside the City Hall. Families can stroll through the market's illuminated park, where each tree is decorated with holiday lights and themes, adding to the magical atmosphere.

4. Tivoli Gardens Christmas Market – Copenhagen, Denmark

Tivoli Gardens in Copenhagen transforms into a winter wonderland with sparkling lights, Scandinavian Christmas decorations, and rides that cater to children. The market features a cozy Santa's grotto, live performances, and a variety of holiday-themed rides. Tivoli's famous wooden roller coaster and carousel add to the thrill, making this market a favorite for families.

5. Grote Markt – Brussels, Belgium

Brussels' Christmas market, set in the beautiful Grand Place, includes an ice rink, Ferris wheel, and light and sound shows. The market offers a kid-friendly atmosphere with rides and attractions specifically designed for families. The light show on the Town Hall is a highlight, with festive music and colorful lights illuminating the historic square.

6. Striezelmarkt – Dresden, Germany

One of the oldest Christmas markets in Europe, Dresden's Striezelmarkt is famous for its traditional charm and family-friendly activities. The market's fairy-tale castle, storytelling corner, and puppet theatre make it ideal for children. There's also a bakery where kids can decorate their own gingerbread cookies and learn about the history of German holiday treats.

7. Old Town Square Christmas Market – Prague, Czech Republic

Prague's Christmas market, located in the city's historic Old Town Square, is a favorite for families. The market includes an animal petting area, an impressive Christmas tree, and a stage for live performances. Children can watch traditional Czech holiday plays and enjoy the chance to ride on a festive carousel.

3. Tips for Parents: Making the Most of Your Visit

With a bit of planning, parents can ensure that their children have a safe and enjoyable experience at the Christmas markets. Here are some tips to help make your visit stress-free and memorable.

Dress Warmly and Comfortably: European winter weather can be chilly, so dressing in layers is essential. Make sure children are bundled up in warm coats, hats, gloves, and scarves. Waterproof boots are also a good idea, especially if the market has ice rinks or outdoor attractions. Bring extra layers for kids who might get cold easily, as well as small hand warmers for added comfort.

Plan Your Visit During Off-Peak Hours:
Christmas markets can become crowded, especially in the evening and on weekends. To give children a bit more space to explore, try visiting during quieter hours, such as weekday mornings or early afternoons. This can help reduce wait times for popular attractions and make it easier for children to enjoy the sights and sounds.

Keep Kids Engaged with a "Market Scavenger Hunt": Turn your visit into a game by creating a scavenger hunt for kids. Challenge them to find certain decorations, foods, or holiday items around the market. For example, you could ask them to find a nutcracker figure, a gingerbread man, or a sparkling star ornament. This activity keeps children entertained and encourages them to explore.

Bring Snacks and Water: Although Christmas markets are filled with delicious treats, children may need quick snacks or water in between activities.

Pack a few healthy snacks, like fruit or granola bars, and a water bottle to keep kids hydrated and energized. This can help prevent hunger-induced meltdowns and give you more time to explore.

Set a Meeting Point: In case anyone gets separated, it's a good idea to establish a meeting point when you first arrive at the market. Pick a distinctive landmark, such as the entrance gate or a large Christmas tree, so that everyone knows where to go if they become separated. For younger children, consider using a safety wristband with your contact information.

Let Kids Choose One or Two Souvenirs: Allowing children to pick out a special souvenir, such as an ornament or a small craft, makes the visit more memorable. Give them a budget and encourage them to find an item that represents their favorite part of the market. This not only makes the experience personal but also helps teach budgeting in a fun way.

Capture the Memories: Christmas markets offer plenty of photo opportunities, so make sure to capture the special moments. Take photos with Santa, in front of the market's main Christmas tree, or during a family ice skating session. These memories will be cherished long after the holiday season is over.

4. Creating Lasting Memories at Family-Friendly Markets

Christmas markets are an ideal setting for creating lasting family memories. With their combination of festive decorations, interactive activities, and enchanting holiday spirit, they offer a holiday experience that's as enjoyable for children as it is for adults. By choosing family-friendly markets and following some practical tips, parents can ensure that their kids have a safe, fun, and unforgettable adventure.

From meeting Santa to enjoying a ride on a festive Ferris wheel, Europe's family-friendly Christmas markets provide countless moments of joy. These magical destinations offer more than just shopping—they create an atmosphere that captures the wonder of the holiday season, making it a truly special experience for families.

Chapter 16

Itinerary Ideas for a Memorable Holiday Market Tour

Planning a Christmas market tour across Europe can be both exciting and overwhelming. With so many enchanting destinations, choosing a route that balances festive charm with practical logistics is essential for a memorable experience. In this chapter, we'll provide sample itineraries designed to help you explore Europe's most magical markets, from immersive week-long stays in Germany or Austria to multi-country routes that capture the spirit of the season across borders. These itineraries cover key details on timing, travel logistics, and must-see activities at each destination, allowing you to focus on soaking in the holiday magic.

1. Classic Christmas in Germany and Austria: A Week-Long Tour

Germany and Austria are home to some of Europe's most iconic Christmas markets, and this itinerary provides a rich experience in just one week. Perfect for those wanting a deep dive into traditional holiday festivities, this route focuses on renowned markets in Germany's Bavaria region and Austria's scenic cities.

Day 1-2: Nuremberg, Germany

- **Highlights:** Start your tour in Nuremberg, home to the famous Christkindlesmarkt. This historic market, with its red-and-white stalls, offers artisanal crafts, mulled wine, and the renowned Nuremberg sausages.
- **Activities:** Visit the Children's Market for family-friendly rides, indulge in gingerbread, and explore Nuremberg Castle for panoramic city views.
- **Travel Tip:** Fly into Nuremberg or take a train from major German cities. Staying in the old town area allows easy access to the market.

Day 3-4: Munich, Germany

- **Highlights:** A short train ride from Nuremberg, Munich's Christkindlmarkt at Marienplatz is a must-see. The market is set against the neo-Gothic City Hall, creating a picture-perfect holiday atmosphere.
- **Activities:** Enjoy traditional German treats like stollen, watch woodcarving demonstrations, and attend the Christmas concert held at the City Hall.
- **Travel Tip:** Munich has multiple Christmas markets, so consider visiting the medieval market in Wittelsbacherplatz for a unique experience.

Day 5-6: Salzburg, Austria

- **Highlights:** Cross the border into Austria with a scenic train ride to Salzburg, known for its romantic holiday atmosphere and the Salzburg Christkindlmarkt.
- **Activities:** Take a tour of the birthplace of Mozart, enjoy Austrian delicacies like sachertorte and krapfen, and attend a choir performance at the Salzburg Cathedral.
- **Travel Tip:** Salzburg is compact, making it easy to explore the market on foot. Don't

miss a day trip to the nearby Hellbrunn Christmas Market, set in palace gardens.

Day 7: Vienna, Austria

- **Highlights:** End your week in Vienna, where Christmas markets light up the city's elegant squares. The Wiener Christkindlmarkt in front of City Hall is particularly magical.
- **Activities:** Stroll through the illuminated Rathauspark, sample Viennese pastries, and shop for handmade ornaments. Wrap up the evening by ice skating at the Rathausplatz ice rink.
- **Travel Tip:** Vienna's markets are spread out, so plan your time to visit key markets like Belvedere Palace and Karlsplatz.

2. Multi-Country Route: Germany, France, and Switzerland (10 Days)

This itinerary covers three countries, each offering its own unique take on holiday traditions. This multi-country tour is ideal for travelers looking to experience diverse cultures and scenery while exploring Europe's festive markets.

Day 1-3: Strasbourg, France

- **Highlights:** Start in Strasbourg, the "Capital of Christmas," where the city's historic center transforms into a winter wonderland.
- **Activities:** Visit the famous Christkindelsmärik, sample Alsatian treats like bredele (Christmas cookies), and take a boat tour along the illuminated canals.
- **Travel Tip:** Strasbourg is well-connected by train. Consider staying in the Petite France district for an authentic experience.

Day 4-6: Freiburg, Germany

- **Highlights:** A short journey from Strasbourg, Freiburg's Christmas market offers a cozy, traditional German holiday experience.
- **Activities:** Try Flammkuchen (German-style pizza), enjoy local wine, and explore the Black Forest for a snowy day trip.
- **Travel Tip:** Freiburg's market is compact and walkable, making it easy to explore the stalls and surrounding sites.

Day 7-8: Basel, Switzerland

- **Highlights:** Basel's Christmas market, set along Barfüsserplatz and Münsterplatz, is one of Switzerland's largest and most beautiful.

- **Activities:** Admire intricate candle making, enjoy Swiss fondue, and visit the Basel Minster for panoramic views.
- **Travel Tip:** Basel is located on the borders of Germany, France, and Switzerland, making it easy to reach by train from neighboring countries.

Day 9-10: Zurich, Switzerland

- **Highlights:** End your tour in Zurich, known for its festive lights and the enchanting Christmas village at Sechseläutenplatz.
- **Activities:** Browse Swiss-made gifts, see the Swarovski tree in Zurich's main train station, and visit the city's fondue chalets.
- **Travel Tip:** Zurich's markets are spread out; use public transport to explore different areas and see the city's renowned holiday lights.

3. Scandinavian Winter Wonderland: 7-Day Tour

For a unique take on holiday markets, consider a Scandinavian itinerary. With cozy markets and the chance to see the Northern Lights, this week-long route offers a blend of festive charm and winter adventure.

Day 1-2: Copenhagen, Denmark

- **Highlights:** Begin in Copenhagen at the Tivoli Gardens Christmas Market, a fairytale setting with Scandinavian holiday decor.
- **Activities:** Enjoy Danish pastries, ride the park's Ferris wheel, and explore the cozy stalls selling handcrafted gifts.
- **Travel Tip:** Copenhagen is compact, and Tivoli Gardens is within walking distance from the city center.

Day 3-4: Gothenburg, Sweden

- **Highlights:** Travel to Gothenburg, known for its Liseberg Christmas Market, which features Sweden's largest Christmas tree and an enchanting Nordic atmosphere.
- **Activities:** Sample Swedish glögg (mulled wine), enjoy ice skating, and see traditional Nordic crafts.
- **Travel Tip:** Consider staying in the city center to enjoy the lights and events that spread across Gothenburg.

Day 5-7: Rovaniemi, Finland

- **Highlights:** End your Scandinavian adventure in Rovaniemi, the official home of Santa Claus, located in the heart of Finnish Lapland.
- **Activities:** Meet Santa, enjoy reindeer sleigh rides, and explore the Santa Claus Village. Try your luck at spotting the Northern Lights in the evenings.
- **Travel Tip:** Rovaniemi is a quick flight from Sweden or Denmark, and the town has plenty of winter activities suitable for all ages.

4. The Grand European Christmas Market Tour: 2 Weeks

For travelers with more time, this itinerary covers a diverse selection of Europe's most iconic Christmas markets across five countries. Ideal for those wanting a full immersion into European holiday traditions, this tour offers stops at markets in Germany, Austria, the Czech Republic, Hungary, and Poland.

Days 1-3: Berlin, Germany

- **Highlights:** Start in Berlin, where you can explore multiple markets like Gendarmenmarkt and Charlottenburg Palace.
- **Activities:** Enjoy Berlin's culinary treats, from currywurst to roasted chestnuts, and browse local crafts at the artisan market.
- **Travel Tip:** Berlin's markets are vast; consider using the metro to reach different markets around the city.

Days 4-6: Prague, Czech Republic

- **Highlights:** Travel to Prague and experience the magic of its Old Town Square Christmas Market.
- **Activities:** Savor traditional Czech pastries, marvel at the nativity scenes, and stroll along the Charles Bridge for festive views.
- **Travel Tip:** Prague's markets are best explored by foot, allowing you to fully enjoy the city's medieval charm.

Days 7-9: Vienna, Austria

- **Highlights:** Spend three days in Vienna, allowing time to explore multiple markets and the city's historic sights.
- **Activities:** Visit the Belvedere Palace market, try Viennese sausages, and attend a classical concert to round out your stay.
- **Travel Tip:** Vienna's public transport makes it easy to visit markets across the city.

Days 10-12: Budapest, Hungary

- **Highlights:** Budapest's Christmas markets are known for their rich holiday traditions and scenic Danube backdrop.
- **Activities:** Sample Hungarian chimney cake, soak in the city's thermal baths, and watch folk dance performances at Vörösmarty Square.
- **Travel Tip:** The Budapest Card offers discounts on transport and select market activities, making it a budget-friendly option.

Days 13-14: Kraków, Poland

- **Highlights:** Conclude your tour in Kraków's Rynek Główny market, set in a historic square with stunning architecture.
- **Activities:** Enjoy Polish pierogi, browse amber jewelry, and listen to the bugle call from St. Mary's Basilica.
- **Travel Tip:** End your trip with a guided tour of Kraków's medieval sites and the nearby Wieliczka Salt Mine for a unique holiday experience.

Planning Your Own Itinerary: Tips and Logistics

Each of these itineraries can be customized based on your time frame and interests. Here are a few tips for planning your journey:

- **Travel by Train:** Europe's train system is extensive, comfortable, and often scenic, making it an ideal way to travel between markets.
- **Choose Shoulder Dates:** Traveling in early December or after Christmas can help you avoid crowds, allowing a more relaxed experience while still enjoying the festive

atmosphere. Many markets open in late November, giving early visitors a chance to explore without peak-season crowds. Similarly, some markets remain open until New Year's, offering post-Christmas travelers a festive experience without the holiday rush.

- **Mix Big Cities with Small Towns:** While major cities like Berlin, Vienna, and Prague are famed for their grand markets, smaller towns often provide a cozier, less commercialized feel. Adding stops in places like Rothenburg ob der Tauber in Germany or Hallstatt in Austria can balance out your itinerary, providing a mix of iconic experiences and hidden gems.

- **Plan for Market Closures:** Some markets close on certain holidays or have limited hours on specific days, especially around Christmas and New Year's. Research each destination's schedule in advance to avoid disappointments and ensure your plans align with local traditions.

- **Pack for Varying Climates:** Winter weather across Europe can be unpredictable. While some markets, especially in northern and eastern Europe, may have snow-covered stalls, others in southern areas might be milder. Packing layers and weather-resistant outerwear is essential for staying comfortable as you explore.

- **Book Accommodations Early:** Christmas markets are incredibly popular, and accommodations in cities like Vienna, Prague, and Strasbourg often book up months in advance. Securing your lodgings early will ensure better options and pricing, especially if you're staying near market areas.

- **Embrace Local Transportation:** Many European cities have efficient public transport systems that make it easy to reach various markets. Consider using day passes, which allow unlimited travel on public buses, trams, and metros and provide a budget-friendly way to navigate the city without the stress of parking.

- **Allow Time for Exploration:** While having a structured itinerary is helpful, leave space for spontaneity. Wandering the festive streets, discovering local cafes, or joining impromptu holiday events can be some of the most memorable moments on your journey.

Conclusion: Crafting a Holiday Market Experience to Cherish

Whether you're exploring the historic markets of Germany, the romantic settings in France, or the snow-dusted stalls of Scandinavia, a European Christmas market tour offers a one-of-a-kind way to celebrate the holiday season. Each itinerary in this chapter presents a curated journey filled with festive delights, cultural immersion, and unforgettable scenery.

By choosing destinations that suit your travel style, planning with logistics in mind, and embracing the unique traditions of each market, you'll create a holiday experience that goes beyond shopping and sightseeing. It's a celebration of warmth, community, and timeless winter traditions—a journey that will fill your heart with the spirit of the season and leave you with cherished memories to savor for years to come.

Chapter 17

Traveling Sustainably: Eco-Friendly Holiday Market Tips

The Importance of Sustainable Tourism

Christmas markets are beloved for their traditional charm, festive ambiance, and local flavor. However, the influx of holiday travelers can have a significant environmental impact, from increased waste to carbon emissions. By adopting eco-friendly practices, visitors can help preserve these cherished markets for generations to come while also making a positive impact on local communities. This chapter offers practical tips to help you enjoy Christmas markets sustainably, ensuring that your holiday experience is both joyful and environmentally responsible.

Sustainable Shopping at Christmas Markets

One of the highlights of Christmas markets is the array of handmade gifts, crafts, and specialty foods. However, sustainable shopping means being mindful of what you buy and the impact it has.

1. Choose Locally Made Gifts

Supporting local artisans not only contributes to the local economy but also reduces the environmental impact associated with importing goods. When selecting gifts, look for items that are handmade by local craftspeople, such as woolen scarves, pottery, wooden toys, or ornaments made from natural materials. These items often have a lower carbon footprint and reflect the unique culture and traditions of the region.

2. Avoid Single-Use Plastics

Many Christmas markets have shifted to using compostable or recyclable materials, but it's still common to encounter single-use plastics. Bring your own reusable bag for shopping, and say no to plastic bags offered by vendors. Additionally, avoid items with excessive plastic packaging, opting instead for unwrapped or minimally packaged goods that are easy to carry.

3. Select Timeless Gifts over Trendy Souvenirs

A sustainable gift is one that will be treasured for years to come. Instead of choosing trendy or seasonal items that may go out of style, select classic, high-quality gifts that friends and family can use or display year after year. This reduces waste and contributes to a more sustainable shopping culture.

Reducing Waste During Your Visit

Christmas markets are often bustling with stalls offering seasonal food, drinks, and snacks, many of which can generate waste. With a few simple steps, you can minimize your environmental impact while enjoying holiday treats.

1. Bring a Reusable Cup and Utensils

If you plan to sample mulled wine, hot chocolate, or other beverages, consider bringing a reusable cup. Many markets offer cups for a deposit fee, but having your own container can reduce waste even further. Likewise, carrying a reusable fork, spoon, or straw can help you avoid single-use cutlery when sampling market foods.

2. Opt for Compostable or Biodegradable Options

In recent years, many Christmas markets have started offering biodegradable plates, cups, and utensils. Be mindful to dispose of these items correctly by looking for designated bins. If you're unsure, ask a vendor about the proper disposal method, as compostable materials should be separated from general waste to break down effectively.

3. Choose Food Portions Wisely

It's easy to get carried away with all the delicious holiday treats, but be mindful to only order what you can finish. Avoiding food waste not only reduces your environmental footprint but also allows you to fully savor each treat. Many markets offer smaller sample portions or shared platters so you can try a variety without creating excess waste.

Supporting Local and Sustainable Businesses

A key part of sustainable travel is supporting businesses that prioritize environmental and social responsibility. By making conscious choices about where to spend your money, you can support those working toward a more sustainable future.

1. Research Vendors and Market Initiatives

Many Christmas markets now feature eco-friendly or fair-trade vendors who are committed to ethical production practices. Look for stalls selling organic products, fair-trade goods, or items made from recycled or upcycled materials. By choosing these vendors, you're supporting businesses that prioritize sustainable production methods.

2. Support Social Enterprises

Some markets include vendors from social enterprises, such as cooperatives that support marginalized communities or organizations that employ people with disabilities. Buying from these stalls not only gives you a unique, meaningful gift but also contributes to positive social change.

3. Opt for Vegan and Vegetarian Food Options

Animal agriculture has a significant environmental impact, so choosing plant-based foods can reduce your carbon footprint. Many Christmas markets now offer a range of vegan and vegetarian dishes, from vegetable-based soups to dairy-free pastries. These options are often just as delicious and provide an eco-friendly way to enjoy local flavors.

Eco-Friendly Travel and Transportation Tips

Sustainable travel goes beyond what you buy; it also includes how you get to and from Christmas markets. By choosing greener modes of transportation, you can reduce your overall environmental impact.

1. Use Public Transportation or Walk

Where possible, opt for public transportation or walk between markets to minimize emissions. Many European cities have excellent public transport systems, and holiday markets are often centrally located. Consider buying a day pass for unlimited travel on buses, trams, and trains, making it easier and more affordable to visit multiple markets sustainably.

2. Carpool or Choose Electric Options

If public transportation isn't an option, consider carpooling with friends or family to reduce emissions. Some cities now offer electric car rental options, which can be a more eco-friendly alternative to traditional gas-powered vehicles. Additionally, many cities in Europe have bike-sharing services or electric scooters that offer a fun, low-emission way to explore.

3. Take the Train for Long-Distance Travel

Train travel is a low-emission way to journey between cities and countries. Europe's extensive rail network makes it easy to plan a holiday market tour using regional trains. Many train companies offer holiday discounts or multi-day passes, allowing you to visit multiple destinations in an eco-friendly manner.

Tips for Being a Responsible Tourist

As a visitor, adopting responsible habits can help protect the environment and respect local communities. By being mindful of your actions, you can contribute to a positive impact on the places you visit.

1. Respect Local Recycling Practices

Each country has its own recycling system, and it's helpful to familiarize yourself with the guidelines. In some cities, waste is separated by type (e.g., paper, glass, compost), and putting items in the wrong bin can lead to contamination. Look for recycling bins in public areas, and if you're unsure, ask locals or vendors for guidance.

2. Limit Energy Use in Accommodations

In hotels or rental accommodations, be mindful of your energy consumption. Simple actions like turning off lights, heating, or air conditioning when you leave can make a difference. Choose eco-friendly accommodations when possible, as many hotels and lodges now participate in green initiatives, such as using renewable energy or offering guests the option to skip daily linen changes.

3. Preserve the Atmosphere of Local Sites

Christmas markets are often held in historic squares or scenic locations that require special care. Be mindful not to damage or litter in these areas, respecting the ambiance that makes them so special. Enjoying the festive atmosphere responsibly helps protect these sites and ensures future generations can experience the same joy.

Conclusion: Embracing Sustainability for a Greener Holiday Experience

A visit to Europe's Christmas markets can be a magical holiday experience, filled with cherished traditions, local culture, and festive cheer. By incorporating sustainable practices into your trip, you can enjoy all the joys of the season while minimizing your environmental impact. From mindful shopping and eco-friendly transportation to supporting local artisans and respecting local customs, every small action counts toward a greener, more responsible holiday.

Traveling sustainably doesn't mean sacrificing comfort or enjoyment—it's about making thoughtful choices that benefit both you and the places you visit. By embracing these eco-friendly tips, you'll not only create lasting memories but also leave a positive legacy that preserves the magic of Christmas markets for years to come.

Chapter 18

Beyond the Markets: Winter Attractions Across Europe

Expanding Your Holiday Adventure

While Europe's Christmas markets are enchanting and memorable, the winter season across the continent offers so much more to explore. From fairytale castles dusted in snow to world-class ski resorts and cultural festivals, Europe is brimming with attractions that make for an unforgettable holiday adventure. This chapter guides you through some of the best winter attractions beyond the markets, including historical landmarks, festive celebrations, and seasonal activities that complement a holiday market tour.

Discovering Enchanting Castles and Historic Sites

Europe is famous for its historic castles, many of which look particularly magical when surrounded by winter landscapes. These majestic sites offer a glimpse into the continent's rich history and architectural beauty, providing an immersive experience for those looking to add a touch of fantasy to their winter travels.

1. Neuschwanstein Castle, Germany

Located in Bavaria, Neuschwanstein Castle is one of the most iconic castles in the world and a must-see in winter. The snow-covered surroundings give it a magical, fairytale-like appearance, making it feel like a scene from a storybook. Nearby towns like Füssen offer cozy accommodations, and you can reach the castle via scenic winter hikes or horse-drawn carriage rides.

2. Château de Chambord, France

In the Loire Valley, Château de Chambord stands as a stunning example of Renaissance architecture. Visiting this castle during winter allows you to avoid the crowds of summer, giving you a more intimate experience. Many nearby towns, like Amboise and

Blois, have holiday markets of their own, allowing you to combine castle visits with seasonal festivities.

3. Edinburgh Castle, Scotland

Perched atop a hill overlooking the Scottish capital, Edinburgh Castle is a remarkable destination, especially in the winter months. The castle's medieval architecture and breathtaking views make it a popular stop for history enthusiasts. Visiting during Edinburgh's winter festivals, such as Hogmanay, adds an extra layer of excitement and cultural immersion.

Experiencing the Thrill of European Ski Resorts

For travelers looking to add an element of adventure to their holiday, Europe's ski resorts offer excellent slopes, stunning mountain views, and cozy après-ski experiences. Whether you're a beginner or an experienced skier, Europe has resorts to suit all levels and preferences.

1. St. Moritz, Switzerland

Famous for its luxury and elegance, St. Moritz is a top destination for skiing enthusiasts and those seeking an upscale winter retreat. Known for hosting the Winter Olympics twice, this Swiss resort offers world-class slopes and high-end accommodations. In addition to skiing, visitors can enjoy the frozen lake's ice-skating rinks, snow polo matches, and gourmet dining.

2. Kitzbühel, Austria

Nestled in the Austrian Alps, Kitzbühel is one of Europe's oldest and most charming ski resorts. Beyond skiing, the town's medieval architecture and winter festivities make it a wonderful place to explore. Don't miss the annual Hahnenkamm ski race, where you can witness some of the world's top skiers competing on one of the most challenging downhill courses.

3. Chamonix-Mont-Blanc, France

As one of the oldest ski resorts in Europe, Chamonix-Mont-Blanc offers breathtaking views of Mont Blanc and attracts visitors from around the world. In addition to skiing and snowboarding, visitors can enjoy scenic train rides, snowshoeing, and visits to the stunning Mer de Glace glacier. The town's vibrant après-ski scene, filled with cozy bars and restaurants, makes it a memorable destination for winter adventurers.

Exploring Cultural Events and Winter Festivals

Many European cities and towns celebrate the winter season with unique cultural events, adding depth and vibrancy to holiday travels. From light festivals to traditional New Year's Eve celebrations, these events offer insight into local customs and are an exciting way to experience Europe's diverse winter traditions.

1. Amsterdam Light Festival, Netherlands

During winter, Amsterdam hosts a spectacular light festival where international artists create illuminated displays along the city's canals. Taking a canal boat tour allows visitors to view these installations up close while enjoying the city's charming architecture. The festival typically runs from December to January, providing a unique experience alongside Amsterdam's Christmas markets.

2. Hogmanay in Edinburgh, Scotland

Scotland's Hogmanay festival is one of the most famous New Year's celebrations in the world, known for its lively atmosphere and traditional customs. The multi-day event includes torchlight processions, live concerts, and a breathtaking fireworks display over Edinburgh Castle. Join in the tradition of "first-footing," where locals and visitors alike bring gifts to friends' and family members' homes to mark the New Year.

3. Carnival of Venice, Italy

For those staying in Europe through the end of January or early February, Venice's Carnival offers a unique and colorful celebration. Known for its elaborate masks, costumes, and masquerade balls, the Carnival brings a sense of mystery and pageantry to Venice's streets. While Venice doesn't have traditional Christmas markets, the Carnival is an unforgettable event that combines history, art, and performance.

Unmissable Winter Attractions and New Year's Celebrations

For travelers seeking a vibrant, festive atmosphere, Europe's New Year's celebrations offer unique events that showcase local customs, cuisine, and entertainment.

1. New Year's Eve in Berlin, Germany

Berlin hosts one of the largest New Year's Eve celebrations in Europe, attracting thousands of visitors each year. The Brandenburg Gate becomes the centerpiece of the festivities, with live music, food stalls, and a midnight fireworks display. For those seeking a lively, urban celebration, Berlin is an excellent choice.

2. Reykjavik's Fireworks Extravaganza, Iceland

In Reykjavik, Icelanders celebrate New Year's Eve with a stunning fireworks display that illuminates the winter sky. Bonfires are lit around the city, creating a cozy yet thrilling atmosphere. For the chance to experience the Northern Lights alongside the New Year's festivities, Reykjavik is an unforgettable destination.

3. La Festa di San Silvestro, Rome, Italy

In Rome, La Festa di San Silvestro is a traditional New Year's Eve celebration that involves live music, fireworks, and festive gatherings in historic locations like Piazza del Popolo. Enjoy an Italian feast with local dishes, then take part in the countdown with locals as the city rings in the New Year with style.

Other Winter Activities to Enhance Your Holiday Experience

Apart from skiing and historic sightseeing, Europe offers a wealth of other winter activities that can complement a Christmas market tour.

1. Ice Skating in Iconic Locations

Ice skating is a popular winter pastime in Europe, and many cities set up rinks in iconic locations. In Paris, the Eiffel Tower and Hôtel de Ville are popular ice-skating spots, offering an unforgettable backdrop. Vienna's City Hall Square and London's Somerset House also feature scenic ice rinks, allowing visitors to glide across the ice while surrounded by stunning architecture.

2. Dog Sledding in Scandinavia

For a unique winter experience, head to Scandinavia for a dog sledding adventure. Norway, Sweden, and Finland all offer dog sledding tours through snow-covered forests and open tundras, where you can learn about traditional Sámi culture and even spot reindeer in the wild. Many tours provide winter gear and instruction, making it accessible for all skill levels.

3. Thermal Baths and Spas

Europe has numerous thermal baths and spas, ideal for relaxing after a day of sightseeing or holiday shopping. In Budapest, the Széchenyi Thermal Bath offers outdoor hot pools where you can soak under the winter sky. Switzerland's St. Moritz and Austria's Bad Gastein also boast world-renowned spa resorts, allowing visitors to unwind and rejuvenate in luxurious, healing waters.

Creating a Balanced Itinerary for the Ultimate Winter Journey

With so many attractions to explore, creating a well-rounded itinerary can help you make the most of your holiday season. Here are a few tips for crafting a winter adventure that combines Christmas markets with other seasonal experiences:

1. Combine City and Countryside Destinations

Balance your trip by pairing city-based Christmas markets with excursions to nearby rural areas or mountain resorts. For instance, visit Munich's holiday markets, then head to the Bavarian Alps for skiing or a castle tour. In France, enjoy Parisian

Christmas markets and then spend a few days exploring the Loire Valley's châteaux.

2. Consider Travel Logistics and Winter Weather

Winter weather can impact travel times and accessibility, especially in rural or mountainous areas. Plan for potential delays, and consider staying longer in certain locations to reduce travel stress. If you're visiting multiple countries, consider using Europe's high-speed trains, which offer a comfortable and scenic way to reach holiday destinations without the hassle of winter driving.

3. Set Aside Time for Relaxation and Reflection

While it's exciting to explore all the festivities, give yourself time to relax and enjoy the holiday season at a leisurely pace. Whether it's an afternoon at a spa, a quiet walk through a snowy park, or a candle-lit evening at a cozy café, these moments of rest allow you to appreciate the magic of winter in Europe.

An Unforgettable European Winter Journey

Europe's Christmas markets are just the beginning of what makes the continent a captivating winter destination. With historic sites, outdoor activities, cultural festivals, and iconic New Year's celebrations, a European holiday tour offers endless possibilities for discovery and joy. By exploring beyond the markets, you'll create a well-rounded, memorable experience that combines the warmth of holiday traditions with the beauty of Europe's winter landscapes. Whether it's skiing in the Alps, celebrating Hogmanay in Edinburgh, or marveling at the lights of Amsterdam, these winter attractions ensure your European holiday journey is truly unforgettable

Conclusion

Embracing the Magic of European Christmas Markets

As the final chapter draws to a close, we hope you feel inspired to embark on a journey that combines the joy of the holiday season with the beauty and diversity of Europe. Christmas markets across the continent offer something truly magical—a blend of festive cheer, local traditions, and the universal warmth that the holiday season brings. Each market is a celebration of both the past and present, weaving together stories of heritage and community that have been cherished for generations.

Celebrate Tradition and Create New Memories

Exploring Europe's Christmas markets is not only a chance to enjoy beautiful sights, sounds, and flavors but also an opportunity to connect with traditions that embody the heart of European culture. Whether you're admiring the craftsmanship of handmade ornaments in Germany, savoring Italian panettone, or sharing mulled wine with locals in the heart of France, you're stepping into moments of celebration that have stood the test of time. Let these traditions enhance your travels and help you discover the unique character of each destination.

At the same time, holiday market travel creates a space for personal memories that will be uniquely yours. From laughter-filled evenings under twinkling lights to quiet reflections in historic town squares, these experiences become a part of your own holiday story. Take the time to savor these moments, capturing them in photos or journals, and allow yourself to be swept up in the wonder of the season.

Final Tips for a Joyous, Stress-Free Holiday Market Journey

As you set out on this festive adventure, keep a few final travel tips in mind to ensure a memorable and stress-free experience:

- **Plan and Pace Yourself**: Christmas markets are filled with things to see and do, so try not to rush through the experience. Set aside enough time for each market, allowing yourself to linger and enjoy the atmosphere without feeling hurried.

- **Embrace Local Customs**: Every Christmas market has its own rhythm and traditions, and embracing these customs can deepen your experience. Take part in local holiday traditions, try traditional foods, and engage with artisans to gain a richer understanding of each culture.
- **Stay Warm and Comfortable**: Dress warmly and wear comfortable shoes to ensure you can fully enjoy every moment. Many markets are best explored on foot, and winter weather can be unpredictable. Staying warm allows you to immerse yourself without distraction.
- **Shop Mindfully**: Holiday markets offer a wealth of handmade gifts and local specialties, perfect for souvenirs or gifts. Support local artisans by choosing authentic, handmade items and consider the story each piece carries. These souvenirs will become treasured reminders of your journey.
- **Capture the Spirit**: Take photos of the scenes that capture your heart—the bustling market stalls, the intricate decorations, or the laughter of loved ones. These images will bring you back to the magic of your journey long after the season has passed.

Well Wishes for an Unforgettable Holiday

As you prepare to embark on your European Christmas market journey, may you carry with you a spirit of joy, wonder, and appreciation. The holiday season is a time for togetherness and gratitude, and Europe's Christmas markets embody these values in their purest form. May your travels be filled with warmth, kindness, and moments of inspiration.

Wherever you roam, remember that the true heart of the holiday season lies in the people you meet, the traditions you embrace, and the memories you create. Let each market visit remind you of the joy of exploration, the beauty of diversity, and the magic of the holiday season. From all corners of Europe, may your journey be bright, your heart be full, and your holiday season truly unforgettable.

Safe travels and a joyous holiday season to you and yours!

Appendices

The appendices provide essential information to ensure your European Christmas market journey is smooth, safe, and well-planned. From practical travel resources to key holiday dates, these sections are designed to give you quick access to helpful tips and vital contacts, making your trip preparation seamless. Here, you'll find tools that enhance your holiday market experience, keep you informed, and help you focus on enjoying your festive journey across Europe.

1. European Holiday Calendars

Major Holiday Dates by Country

To help you plan your visit, here is a list of major holiday dates across popular European Christmas market destinations. Many Christmas markets have their busiest days leading up to Christmas Eve, so knowing these dates can help you plan for crowds or find quieter moments.

- **Germany**
    - Advent Sundays (four Sundays before Christmas)

- Christmas Eve: December 24
- Christmas Day: December 25
- Boxing Day: December 26
- **Austria**
  - Advent Sundays
  - St. Nicholas Day: December 6
  - Christmas Eve: December 24
  - Christmas Day: December 25
  - St. Stephen's Day: December 26
- **France**
  - St. Nicholas Day: December 6 (in Alsace)
  - Christmas Eve: December 24
  - Christmas Day: December 25
- **United Kingdom**
  - Christmas Day: December 25
  - Boxing Day: December 26
- **Scandinavia**
  - St. Lucia Day: December 13 (Sweden)
  - Christmas Eve: December 24
  - Christmas Day: December 25
  - Second Day of Christmas: December 26

Use these dates to align your visits with holiday traditions or plan your itinerary around quieter times.

2. Currency and Exchange Tips

Common Currencies

Europe comprises multiple countries with their own currencies. While the Euro (€) is widely used across the continent, several countries still have their own currencies. Here's a quick guide to help you navigate:

- **Euro (€)**: Used in most European countries, including Germany, France, Austria, Italy, and Spain.
- **British Pound (£)**: United Kingdom (GBP)
- **Swiss Franc (CHF)**: Switzerland
- **Danish Krone (DKK)**: Denmark
- **Swedish Krona (SEK)**: Sweden
- **Norwegian Krone (NOK)**: Norway
- **Czech Koruna (CZK)**: Czech Republic
- **Hungarian Forint (HUF)**: Hungary
- **Polish Zloty (PLN)**: Poland

Exchange and Budgeting Tips

- **Exchange Currency in Advance**: It's often cheaper to exchange currency before arriving in Europe. Consider getting some local currency for smaller purchases.

- **Use Credit and Debit Cards**: Credit and debit cards are widely accepted across Europe. Visa and Mastercard are most common; however, always carry some cash for markets and smaller vendors.
- **Avoid Dynamic Currency Conversion**: When using a card, choose to be charged in the local currency rather than your home currency to get a better exchange rate.
- **Budget for Markets**: Plan for extra expenses at Christmas markets, including food, souvenirs, and activities. Allocate funds for each market to avoid overspending.

3. Emergency Contacts

Essential Numbers and Hotlines

Emergencies can happen anywhere, and it's wise to be prepared. Here's a list of essential contacts to keep handy while traveling across Europe:

- **European Union Emergency Number**: 112 (for police, fire, or ambulance in most EU countries)
- **Local Police Numbers**:
    - **Germany**: 110 (Police), 112 (Fire and Ambulance)

- ○ **France**: 17 (Police), 18 (Fire), 15 (Ambulance)
- ○ **United Kingdom**: 999 or 112
- ○ **Switzerland**: 117 (Police), 144 (Ambulance), 118 (Fire)
- **Lost/Stolen Credit Cards**:
  - ○ Visa Global Customer Assistance: +1-303-967-1096
  - ○ Mastercard Assistance Center: +1-636-722-7111
- **Embassies and Consulates**: Locate the contact information for your country's embassy or consulate in each country you visit. Having this on hand can be crucial if you need urgent assistance.

Medical and Travel Insurance Contacts

Ensure you have travel insurance that includes emergency medical assistance. Write down the contact information for your insurer and keep it accessible.

4. Planning Resources

Helpful Websites and Apps: These tools and resources will make your travel experience smoother, providing guidance on everything from transportation to local events:

- **Transportation**:
  - **Rail Europe**: For booking train travel across Europe.
  - **FlixBus**: Affordable bus service in many European countries.
  - **Citymapper**: A public transportation app available in major European cities.
- **Accommodation**:
  - **Booking.com**: Comprehensive options for hotels, apartments, and hostels across Europe.
  - **Airbnb**: Great for unique stays and local experiences.
- **Currency Exchange and Budgeting**:
  - **XE Currency**: Real-time currency converter app.
  - **Trail Wallet**: Budget tracker ideal for travelers.
- **Language Assistance**:
  - **Google Translate**: Language translation app, including offline mode.
  - **Duolingo**: Language-learning app to help you with basic phrases.

- **Event and Holiday Market Info**:
  - ○ **ChristmasMarkets.com**: Information on Christmas market dates and details.
  - ○ **Local Tourism Websites**: Many cities have tourism websites with updated information on holiday events.

Packing Tips for a Comfortable Market Tour

- **Layered Clothing**: Layering is essential for changing temperatures. Base layers, sweaters, and a warm coat will keep you comfortable.
- **Comfortable Shoes**: Most markets involve a lot of walking, so bring comfortable, weather-proof shoes.
- **Reusable Bag**: Great for carrying purchases and reduces waste.
- **Portable Charger**: Capture memories without worrying about battery life.

Sustainable Travel Tips

Make the most of your travels while reducing your environmental impact:

- **Reusable Mug**: Many Christmas markets offer discounts for using your own cup for hot drinks.
- **Limit Plastic Use**: Avoid single-use plastics by bringing a reusable bag and cutlery.
- **Buy Local**: Support local artisans and small businesses at the markets, choosing authentic souvenirs over mass-produced goods.

Conclusively, the appendices offer valuable resources and information to help you navigate your European Christmas market journey with confidence. From important contact numbers to practical travel tips, each section has been thoughtfully included to enhance your holiday experience and ensure your trip goes smoothly. Remember to refer back to these resources as you plan your travels, and don't hesitate to use these tips on the road. With the right preparation, you'll be free to enjoy the enchanting sights, sounds, and flavors of Europe's holiday markets to the fullest.

Safe travels, happy planning, and may your holiday market tour be filled with joy, wonder, and unforgettable memories!